Discovered in 1901 and
re-published at Innsbruck in 1903

By Stefan Zweig

NOVEL

BEWARE OF PITY

BIOGRAPHIES

MASTER BUILDERS: A TYPOLOGY OF THE SPIRIT
one-volume edition of:
Three Masters: Balzac · Dickens · Dostoeffsky
The Struggle with the Daimon: Hölderlin · Kleist · Nietzsche
Adepts in Self-Portraiture: Casanova · Stendhal · Tolstoy

CONQUEROR OF THE SEAS: *The Story of Magellan*

THE RIGHT TO HERESY: *Castellio against Calvin*

MARY QUEEN OF SCOTLAND AND THE ISLES

ERASMUS OF ROTTERDAM

MARIE ANTOINETTE: *The Portrait of an Average Woman*

JOSEPH FOUCHÉ: *The Portrait of a Politician*

MENTAL HEALERS: *Mesmer · Mary Baker Eddy · Freud*

STORIES

AMOK

CONFLICTS

KALEIDOSCOPE

THE BURIED CANDELABRUM

LETTER FROM AN UNKNOWN WOMAN

TRAVEL

BRAZIL: *Land of the Future*

PLAYS

JEREMIAH
VOLPONE (*after Ben Jonson*)

AMERIGO

A Comedy of Errors in History

Nunc vero & heę partes funt latius luſtratæ/ &
alia quarta pars per Americū Vefputium(vt in ſe＊
quentibus audietur)inuenta eſt:quā non video cur
quis iure vetet ab Americo inuentore ſagacis inge
nij viro Amerigen quaſi Americi.terram/ſiue Ame
ricam dicendam:cum & Europa & Aſia a mulieri＊
bus ſua fortita ſint nomina.Eius ſitū & gentis mo＊
res ex bis binis.Americi nauigationibus quę ſequū
tur liquide intelligi datur.

"But now these parts have been more extensively explored and
another fourth part has been discovered by Americus Vespucius
(as will appear in what follows): wherefore I do not see what
is rightly to hinder us from calling it Amerige or America, i.e.
the land of Americus, after its discoverer Americus, a man of
sagacious mind, since both Europe and Asia have got their
names from women. Its situation and the manners and customs
of its people will be clearly understood from the twice two
voyages of Americus which follow."—*John Fiske's translation.*

The paragraph from *Cosmographiæ Introductio* in
which Waldseemüller proposes the name

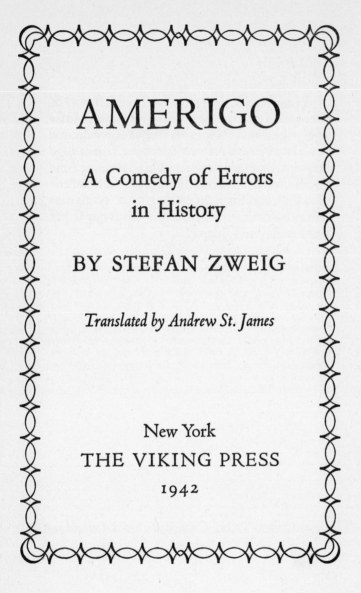

AMERIGO

A Comedy of Errors in History

BY STEFAN ZWEIG

Translated by Andrew St. James

New York

THE VIKING PRESS

1942

This work originally appeared
serially in *Blue Book* under the title,

THE MYSTERY OF AMERICA'S GODFATHER

CONTENTS

ILLUSTRATIONS

I

Amerigo

AFTER whom is America called America? Any child of
school age will answer this question without hesi-
tation: after Amerigo Vespucci. But the second question
will find even adults wavering and uncertain: the question as to why this continent was christened after Amerigo Vespucci's first name. Because Vespucci discovered
America? He never discovered it. Because he was the first
to set foot on the mainland, rather than on the islands
lying before it? No, not for this reason, either, because it
was not Vespucci who was the first to set foot on the new
continent, but Columbus and Sebastian Cabot. Perhaps it
was because he made a deceitful assertion that he was the

first to have landed here? Vespucci never claimed this legal title in any court. Or was it because as a scientist and cartographer he ambitiously suggested his name for the new country? No, he never did this, either; and it is very likely that during his lifetime he never even heard what this continent had been called. But why, if he achieved none of these things, did the honour of having his name immortalized for all time fall just to him? Why was this continent named America, and not Columbia?

How this happened is an endless story of accidents, errors, and misunderstandings—the story of a man who, on the strength of a journey he never undertook, and which he himself never claimed to have undertaken, captured the amazing fame of having his first name used for the fourth continent of our earth. This christening surprised and annoyed the world for four centuries. Over and over again Amerigo Vespucci has been accused of having obtained this honour surreptitiously by ignoble and shady intrigues; and this litigation of "fraud on the grounds of perjury" has been discussed continuously, always before new and learned courts. While some acquitted Vespucci, others condemned him to eternal disgrace; and the more clearly his defendants established his innocence, the more passionately did his adversaries accuse him of lying, forgery, and theft. Today these polemics—with all their hypotheses, proofs, and counter-proofs —fill a whole library. By some, the godfather of America is considered an *amplificator mundi,* one of the great expanders of our world, an explorer, a seafarer, a scientist of the highest rank; by others, the most impertinent impostor or juggler in the history of geography. On which side, then, lies the truth—or, to be more careful—the greatest probability?

Today the case of Vespucci has long since ceased to be a geographical or philological problem. It is a game of conjecture in which any person of curiosity can take part, and withal an easily comprehensible game, played with few men; for the whole literary opus of Vespucci, so far as we know, comprises—all documents included—no more than forty or fifty pages. Thus may I also be permitted to reconstruct once more the figures, and to replay, move for move, with all its surprises and errors, the famous master game of History. The only demand of a geographical nature which my presentation makes on the reader is that he should forget all the geography he has

Amerigo

ever learned from our complete atlases, and erase from the map in his mind's eye the shape, position—yes, even the existence—of America. Only he who is capable of imagining the darkness and uncertainty of that early century will properly appreciate the surprise and enthusiasm of that generation when the first outlines of an undreamt-of continent began to delineate themselves from a world which so far had been considered without end. But wherever humanity recognizes something new, it must needs give that discovery a name. Wherever it feels enthusiasm, its joy seeks to express itself in loud acclamations. Thus it was a happy day when the wind of chance cast a name across humanity's path; and without concern over right or wrong, it impatiently seized upon the glamorous word and greeted its New World with the new and immortal name of America.

2

The Historical Situation

A.D. 1000. A dark and heavy slumber lies over the Western World. The eyes are too drowsy to open wide and look around, the senses too exhausted to be stirred by curiosity. As after a fatal illness, the spirit of mankind is paralysed; it has no desire to know anything more of its world. And what is still stranger, even the knowledge it had acquired had been mysteriously forgotten. It has forgotten how to read, how to write, how to count; even the kings and emperors of the Occident are no longer capable of signing a document with their own names. The sciences have become calcified into theological mummies; the human hand is no longer able to reproduce its own form in drawing or sculpture. An impenetrable fog, as it were, seems to lie over every horizon; no one travels any more, no one knows anything about foreign lands; the populace takes refuge in the fortresses and towns from the savage nations which again and again come invading from the East. Life has grown cramped, limited; men live in the dark, without courage—a dark and heavy slumber lies over the Western World.

Occasionally in this heavy slumber an obscure memory dawns upon men that once upon a time the world was different—larger, brighter, more colourful, filled with action and adventure. Weren't there once roads leading through all countries, roads on which the Roman legions marched, and in their wake the lictors, the representatives of the law, the guardians of justice? Wasn't there once a man named Cæsar, who had conquered both Egypt and Britain? Didn't triremes once sail across to countries on the other side of the Mediterranean, a sea into which no ship for a long time has dared venture for fear of pirates? Wasn't there at one time a King Alexander, who penetrated into that legendary land called India, and returned through Persia? Weren't there once wise men who knew how to read the stars, men cognizant of the shape of the world and of the mysteries of Man? All these things should be studied in books, but books no longer exist. Men ought to travel and see foreign lands, but there are no roads. Everything has disappeared. But perhaps all this was only a dream.

In any case, why take all this trouble? Why exert oneself when everything is coming to an end anyhow? For in the year 1000, so it has been prophesied, the world will perish. God has passed His judgment because mankind has committed too many crimes—such is the preaching of the priests from their pulpits; and on the first day of the year 1000 the Great Judgment is to begin. Bewildered, with their garments rent, people assemble in huge processions, lighted candles in their hands. Peasants leave their fields; the rich squander their fortunes; for tomorrow they are coming, the Horsemen of the Apocalypse on their pale steeds: the Day of Judgment is at hand. Thousands upon thousands spend this last night kneeling in the churches, waiting for the plunge into everlasting darkness.

1100. No, the world has not come to an end. Once more God has taken mercy on mankind. It is allowed to go on living. It must go on living, to prove its goodness and its greatness. He must be thanked for His mercy; humanity must raise its gratitude to Heaven as though with hands in prayer; and so it comes about that domes and cathedrals grow up, these stone pillars of prayer. And mankind must manifest its love for Christ, the mediator of His love and mercy. Can humanity continue to tolerate that the place of His suffering should remain in the hands of the wicked heathens? Up, knights of the Western World! Up, all ye faithful, and on toward the East! Have ye not heard the call: "It is God's Will"? Out, out of the fortresses and villages and towns, and onward, to join the crusade on land and sea!

1200. The Holy Sepulchre is conquered and lost again. The crusade is in vain, and yet not altogether in vain. For Europe has awakened through this adventure. It has felt its own power, has measured its own courage, and has once more discovered how many new and different things have home and place in God's world. Different trees, fruit, people, animals, and customs, under a different sky. Surprised and ashamed, the knights and peasants and serfs recognize in the East how limited and gloomy were their lives at home in their Occidental corner, and how rich, refined, and luxurious are those of the

The Historical Situation

Saracens. These heathens, whom they had despised from afar, have soft smooth fabrics of Indian silk, carpets from Bukhara, glowing with colour; they have spices, herbs, and perfumes, which excite and stimulate the senses. Their ships sail to the farthest lands to fetch slaves, pearls, and gleaming ores; their caravans travel the roads on endless journeys. No, indeed, they are not the wild brigands they had been led to expect; they know the world and its mystery. They have maps and charts on which everything is written and recorded. They have wise men who know the course of the stars, and the laws by which they move. They have conquered countries and seas, have seized for themselves all wealth, all trade, all lust of life, and yet they are no better warriors than the German or the Frankish knights.

But how have they done it? They have learned. They have schools, and in their schools are scripts that communicate and explain everything. They know the lore of the ancient seers of the West and have augmented it by new research. Thus, in order to conquer the world, learning is imperative. Strength must not be dissipated in tourneys and wild festivity; the mind must be made flexible, sharp as the edge of a Toledo sword. So think, learn, study, observe—these are the orders of the day! And with impatient rivalry one university after another appears—in Siena and Salamanca, in Oxford and Toulouse. It is every European country's desire to be the first to excel in knowledge. After centuries of indifference, Western man tries his hand once more at exploring the mysteries of the earth, the heavens, and the human being.

1300. Europe has torn off the theological cowl which obstructed its free outlook on the world. There's no point in always brooding over God, nor any sense in having endless interpretations and discussions on the subject of the old scripts. God is the Creator, and as He has made man after His own image, He wants him to be creative. In all the arts and sciences the models of the Greeks and Romans still remain; perhaps their standard could be reached again; it may be possible to repeat what the knowledge of olden times once achieved. Not impossible, perhaps, that it could be surpassed. A new courage springs up in the Western World. Once more men begin to write poetry, to paint, to philosophize—and, behold! they succeed. They triumph beyond all expectations. A Dante appears and a Giotto, a Roger Bacon and the builders of the Domes. Hardly has the liberated spirit had time to spread its so long-unused wings before its message has gone far and wide.

But why does the world below remain so narrow? Why is the terrestrial, the geographical, world so limited? The sea is everywhere, nothing but sea round every shore, symbolizing the unknown, the unconquerable; everywhere the endless ocean extending beyond the range of human sight, *"ultra nemo scit quid contineatur"*—of which no one knows what it conceals. Only southward leads a road across Egypt to the dreamlands of India, but the way is barred by the heathens. And no mortal man may venture past the Pillars of Hercules, the Strait of Gibraltar. It means the end for ever of all adventure. As Dante says,

> *quella foce stretta*
> *Ov' Ercole segnó li suoi riguardi*
> *Accioché l'uom piu oltre non si metta.*

Ah, no road leads out into the *"mare tenebrosum"*; no ship turning its keel into this dark desert will ever return. Man is destined to live in a world he does not know; he is imprisoned on the earth, whose size and shape will probably never be explored.

1298. Two aged bearded men, accompanied by a young

one, obviously the son of one of them, land by boat in Venice. They are wearing strange garments such as have never been seen on the Rialto—thick coats trimmed with fur, and peculiar ornaments. But stranger still, these three foreigners speak the purest Venetian dialect, claim to be Venetians and to be called Polo, the young one answering to the name of Marco Polo. What they have to relate cannot, of course, be taken seriously—namely, that more than two decades ago they had travelled through the Kingdom of the Muscovites, through Armenia and Turkestan as far as Mange (China), where they had lived at the court of the most powerful ruler on earth, the Kubla Khan. They had travelled across the whole vast country, compared with which Italy was no larger than a flower beside a tree. They had arrived at the edge of the world, where once more there lay an ocean. And when, after many years, the great Khan discharged them, with many gifts, from his service, they had journeyed back on this ocean to their native land—first passing Zipangu and the Spice Islands, the great island of Taprobane (Ceylon), and later sailing through the Persian Gulf, after which they returned safely via Trapezunt.

The Venetians listened to the three men, and laughed.

The Historical Situation

What amusing story-tellers! Never had any Christian worthy of belief reached this farther ocean or set foot on these islands of Zipangu and Taprobane! Impossible. But the Polos invite guests to their house, and there display their presents and jewels. Surprised, the premature sceptics recognize that their countrymen have accomplished the most audacious discovery of their time. Like a fanned fire, their reputation spreads through the Western World, awakening the new hope that it is possible after all to get to India. So these richest regions of the globe can be reached, and from there one can travel further, to the other end of the world!

1400. To reach India—this has now become the dream of the century. And it is the lifelong dream of one single man—Prince Enrique of Portugal, whom history dubs Henry the Navigator, though he himself had never travelled the ocean. But his whole life and aim culminate in this one dream—*"pasar a donde nascen las especerias"* —to reach the Indian islands, the Moluccas, where grow the precious cinnamon, pepper, and ginger for which the merchants of Italy and Flanders of these days pay with gold. The Ottomans have closed the nearest route, the Red Sea, to the "Rumis," the Unbelievers, and seized the lucrative trade as a monopoly. Wouldn't it be a profitable and at the same time a Christian crusade to attack the enemies of the Occident in the rear? Wouldn't it be possible, perhaps, to reach the Spice Islands by sailing round Africa? In the old books there is a strange story of a Phœnician ship which many hundreds of years ago sailed from the Red Sea, round Africa, and returned to Carthage, after two years. Wouldn't it be possible to try this again?

Prince Henry gathers round him the learned men of his day. On Cape Sagres, the south-westernmost point of Portugal, where the vast Atlantic Ocean foams high against the cliffs, he builds himself a castle, where he sets about collecting maps and nautical data. He summons astronomers and pilots, one after another. The older scholars maintain that any attempt to cross the equator would be in vain. They refer to Aristotle, and Strabo, and Ptolemy, the wise men of antiquity. They insist that the water of the sea in the tropical regions would thicken, become a *"mare pigrum,"* and the ships catch fire from the scorching heat of the sun. No man could live in these regions, no tree or vegetation grow there. Mariners' hearts would fail them at sea, and they would starve on land.

The Historical Situation

But there are other scholars, Jews and Arabs, who contradict this. They declare that the venture could be risked, and that these legends were spread only by Moorish merchants in order to discourage the Christians. They went on to say that the great geographer Edrisi had long ago established the fact that in the south a fertile country did exist, Bilad Ghana (Guinea), whence the Moors fetched their black slaves by caravan across the desert. These scholars had seen Arab maps showing the route round Africa, and declared that a journey along the coast could be risked now that the new instruments made it possible to decide the degree of latitude, and the magnetic needle, introduced from China, indicated the directions of the earth's poles. It could be undertaken, they said, provided larger and more seaworthy ships were built. Prince Henry gives commands, and the daring venture gets under way.

1450. The great adventure, the immortal Portuguese feat, has begun. In 1419 Madeira is discovered, or rather rediscovered; in 1435 the long-sought-for "Isolæ Fortunatæ" of antiquity are found. Almost every year brings a fresh advance. Cape Verde has been circumnavigated; in 1445 Senegal is reached—and, behold, everywhere there are palms, fruit, and people! The new era already knows more than did the wise men of the olden days, and while on his expedition Nuno Tristão can triumphantly report —"with the permission of his honour Ptolemæus"!—that he has discovered fertile lands where the great Greek had denied any possibility of it. For the first time in a thousand years a seaman has dared to ridicule the omniscient geographer. Each new hero outwits the other, Diogo Cam and Diniz Diaz, Cadamosto and Nuno Tristão; each one, on a previously untrodden coast, erects the Portuguese cross as a sign of occupation. With amazement the world follows the progress into the unknown of this small nation, which alone achieves the *"feito nunca feito"*—the never-accomplished feat.

1486. Triumph! They have sailed round Africa! Bartolomeu Diaz has sailed round the Cabo Tormentoso, the Cape of Good Hope. From there they cannot continue any further south. Now, all they have to do is to sail eastward, across the ocean, with the aid of favourable monsoons, along the route already described on maps which were brought to the King of Portugal by two Jewish envoys who had been sent to Prester John, the Christian King of Abyssinia—then India is reached. But Bartolomeu Diaz's crew is exhausted, and he is thereby deprived of a feat which Vasco da Gama is to accomplish. But let this be enough for the moment; the way is found; no one can forestall Portugal now.

1492. But they have spoken too soon—someone *has* stolen a march on Portugal. Something unbelievable has happened. A certain Colón, or Colom, or Colombo—*"Christophorus quidam Colonus vir Ligurus,"* as Peter Martyr reports; *"una persona que ninguna persona conocia,"* as another relates—has sailed westward under a Spanish flag into the open ocean, instead of eastward round Africa, and has, on this *"brevissimo cammino,"* according to his own account, performed the miracle of miracles—reached India! Though he has not met Marco Polo's Kubla Khan, he has nevertheless been the first man of all, so he reports, to land on the island of Zipangu (Japan) and later in Mange (China). Had he prolonged his voyage only a few more days, he would have reached the Ganges.

Europe gapes in amazement when Columbus returns with strange red-skinned Indians, with parrots and other peculiar animals, and great tales of gold. Strange, indeed —the globe must after all be smaller than men thought, and Toscanelli must have spoken the truth. Only three weeks' sailing westward from Spain or Portugal, and there one is in China or Japan, and quite near the Spice Islands. So what folly it was for the Portuguese to have travelled six months round Africa, if India with all its treasures lay so close to the gates of Spain. And now the first thing that happens is that Spain, by papal bull, secures for herself this route to the west and all that has been discovered there.

˙ 1493. Columbus—now no longer a certain *"quidam,"* but a great admiral of His Royal Majesty, and viceroy of the newly discovered provinces—sails for the second time to India. On him he has letters from his Queen to the great Khan, whom he hopes this time to meet for certain in China. He is taking with him 1500 men—warriors, sailors, settlers, and even musicians ("to entertain the natives")—as well as plenty of iron-fitted chests for the gold and jewels he intends bringing home from Zipangu and Calicut.

1497. Another seafarer, Sebastian Cabot, has sailed across the ocean from England—and, strangely enough, he also has reached land. Is this the old "Vinland" of the Vikings? Is it China? Whatever it is, wonderful to relate, the ocean, the *"mare tenebrosum,"* is conquered, and must, by degrees, deliver up its secrets to the daring men.

1499. Rejoicing in Portugal, sensation in Europe! Vasco da Gama has returned from India via the dangerous Cape. He has chosen the other, the longer, more difficult route, and has landed in Calicut (where the rich zamorins of legend live), and not, like Columbus, merely on small islands and the remote mainland; for he has actually seen the heart of India and its treasure houses. In no time another expedition is being equipped under Cabral. Spain and Portugal are now competing for India.

1500. A new event. Cabral on his trip round Africa has travelled too far to the west and has again encountered land in the south, as Columbus did in the north. Is this Antilla, the legendary island of the old maps? Or is it India again?

1502. Too many things are happening to be grasped and understood. In this one decade more has been discovered than hitherto in a thousand years. Ship after ship leaves the harbour, each one returning with a new message. It is as though a fog had suddenly been magically wafted away: so long as the prows turn westward, lands and islands appear everywhere, in the north and in the south; and the calendar with all its saints has not sufficient names to christen them all. The admiral Columbus alone claims to have discovered thousands of them, and to have seen rivers whose springs come from Paradise. But how was it that all these islands and strange countries on the Indian coast were unknown to the Arabs and the men of yore? Why did not Marco Polo mention them? Why is everything he reports from Zipangu and Zaitun so different from what the admiral describes? It is all so confusing and contradictory and filled with mystery that men do not know what to believe of these islands in the west. Has the world actually been circumnavigated already? Has Columbus really been so near the Ganges that, coming from the west, he would meet Vasco da Gama sailing from the east? Is the terrestrial globe smaller, or bigger, than had been believed? If only someone would appear to explain all these miracles, now that the German printers had made books so much more easily accessible! The scholars, mariners, merchants, and princes—the whole of Europe is waiting impatiently. After all these discoveries, mankind wants finally to know just what has been discovered. Every single person feels that the decisive feat of the century has been achieved; but the meaning and the explanation are still lacking.

3

Immortality from 32 Pages

IN THE year 1503, almost simultaneously in Paris and Florence, though no one knows definitely in which city they first appeared, four to six printed pages, entitled *Mundus Novus,* were seen bandied about. As the author of this tract, written in Latin, there is mentioned one Albericus Vespucius or Vesputius who, in the form of a letter, reports to Laurentius Petrus Franciscus de Medici about a voyage into hitherto unknown countries undertaken in the service of the King of Portugal. Such reports in letter form concerning a voyage of exploration are not rare at this time. All great trading firms in Germany, Holland, and Italy—the Welsers, Fuggers, Medicis, as well as the Signoria of Venice—have their correspondents in Seville and Lisbon, who report on each successful expedition to India for the purpose of supplying information useful for business. Since these letters of their commercial attachés really tell business secrets, they are very much sought after; and copies of them are placed on the market as objects of value in the same way as are the maps—the portolanos—of newly discovered coasts. Sometimes these copies fall into the hands of a diligent printer who immediately reproduces them on his press. And these pamphlets, which for the large public take the place of the so far non-existent newspaper by making interesting news accessible, are then sold in the fairs, together with letters of indulgence and medical prescriptions. Friends, writing to one another, enclose them in their letters and parcels. Thus an original private letter from a commercial agent to his employer sometimes acquires the publicity of a printed book.

Not since the first letter of Columbus in 1493, announcing his arrival in the islands "near the Ganges," has any one of these pamphlets caused so universal a stir, and one of such consequence, as the four pages of this until now entirely unknown Albericus. Even the subtitle suggests something sensational. It explains that the following letter is *"ex italica in latinam linguam,"* translated from the Italian into Latin, "so that all learned people shall see how many wonderful things are being discovered nowadays" (*"quam multa miranda in dies reperiantur"*); how many so far unknown worlds, and all that they contain, have been found (*"quanto a tanto tempore quo mundus cepit ignota sit vastitas terre e que continetur in ea"*). This resounding announcement in itself is a strong enticement for a world starving for news. The result is that the little pamphlet has a rapid sale. It is reprinted several times in the most remote small towns, is translated into German, Dutch, French, Italian, and included immediately in all anthologies on travel which just now are beginning to appear in every language. It is a landmark, if not the very foundation, of the new geography for the still unsuspected world.

The enormous success of this tiny book is quite comprehensible, for this unknown Vesputius is the first of all navigators to know how to write well and amusingly. Those who usually gather together on these adventure ships are illiterate beachcombers, sailors, and soldiers, who cannot even sign their own names; at best there may be an *"escribano,"* an uninspired scribe capable of little more than stringing together a number of dry facts, or a pilot who makes notes of the degrees of latitude and longitude. Thus, at the turn of the century, the great masses are still entirely uninformed as to what has been discovered in foreign lands. Then, suddenly, there appears a convincing, even learned man, neither exaggerating nor telling tall stories, but honestly describing how, beginning on May 14, 1501, in the service of the King of Portugal, he sailed for two months and two days across the vast ocean under a sky so dark and stormy that neither sun nor moon was visible. Making the reader share all the horrors, he goes on to relate how all hope of a safe landing had been abandoned for the leaking ships, which were already beginning to be eaten away by worms; how, on August 7, 1501 (the date differs from his other reports, but one has to accustom oneself to such inaccuracies from this scholarly man), thanks to his cleverness as cosmographer, they finally spied land—and what a land! A land where men live without work or hardship, where trees need no care, rivers and springs flow with pure water, the sea is full of fish, the soil incredibly fertile, and filled to overflowing with delicious and entirely unknown fruit. Cool breezes stir over this rich land, and the dense forests make even the hottest days enjoyable.

A thousand species of beast and bird, he writes, live there, of whose existence Ptolemy seems to have had no idea. The natives still exist in a state of perfect innocence. They are of a reddish complexion—because, so the traveller explains, all their lives they walk about naked, and thus are burned by the sun. They possess neither clothes, nor ornaments, nor any other property. What they do have belongs to all—not excluding the women, of whose ever-obliging sensuousness the learned gentleman has some rather risky anecdotes to tell. Shame and moral codes, he says, are completely unknown to these children of nature: father sleeps with daughter, brother with sister, and mother with son. Here, there is no such thing as an Œdipus complex, or inhibitions; yet they live to be a hundred and fifty years old—provided, and this seems to be their only unpleasant habit, they do not eat each other before. In short, "if Paradise exists anywhere, it cannot be very far from here." Before Vesputius leaves Brazil—for such is the described Paradise—he indulges in a detailed description of the beauty of the stars, which shine in different constellations over this blessed hemisphere, and ends with a promise to tell more about this and other journeys in a book, so that he "may be remembered by the world to come" *("ut mei recordatio apud posteros vivat")* and also in order to make known "God's wonderful creations in this hitherto unknown part of the world."

It is not difficult to understand the sensation which this lively, colourful report caused among the author's contemporaries. For not only is the curiosity about these unknown regions both stirred and satisfied, but this Vesputius, by asserting that if "Paradise exists anywhere, it cannot be far from here," has touched on one of the most mysterious hopes of his epoch. The Fathers of the Church, especially the Greek theologists, had long ago advanced the theory that God had by no means destroyed Paradise after the Fall of Adam. He had only removed it to the "antiterra," a sphere inaccessible to human beings. According to mythological theology this antiterra was supposed to exist beyond the ocean—that is, in a zone impenetrable by mortals. But now, when the daring of the explorers had caused this uncrossable ocean to be traversed, and they had reached the hemisphere of the

other stars, could not the ancient dream of humanity
after all be fulfilled, and Paradise rewon? It seems only
natural, therefore, that Vesputius's description of this
world of innocence, which strangely resembles the world
before the Fall of Man, should excite an age which, like
our own, is surrounded by catastrophe. In Germany, the
peasants are rioting, because they refuse to tolerate serf-
dom any longer; in Spain the Inquisition is rampant,
allowing no peace or security even to the most harmless
of men; while in Italy and France the land is being rav-
aged by war. Thousands, hundreds of thousands of people, tired of such daily affliction and disgusted with this
crazy world, have already escaped into convents. Nowhere is there calm, rest, or peace for the common man,
who pleads for nothing more than to be allowed to go his
own way unmolested. Then suddenly there comes news,
in the form of a few small leaflets fluttering from town
to town: a trustworthy man—neither swindler, Sindbad,
nor liar—but a learned man, sent by the King of Portugal, who had discovered far beyond the hitherto known
zones a land where there was still peace for mankind, a
land where the struggle for money, property, and power
had not destroyed the soul of man; a country without

princes or kings, without extortioners or slave-drivers,
where it is not necessary for hands to be worked to the
bone for daily bread, where the earth charitably produces
food, and where men are not the eternal enemies of one
another. It is an ancient, religious, Messianic hope which
this unknown Vesputius kindles with his report; he has
touched on the deepest longing of mankind, on the dream
of freedom from customs, money, law, and property; on
the unquenchable desire for life without hardship, without responsibility, which slumbers mysteriously in the
souls of all men, like a dark memory out of Paradise.

This peculiar circumstance may have been the reason
why these few and badly printed leaflets had an effect on
the time surpassing by far all other reports, not excluding
that of Columbus. But the real fame and the world-
historical importance of this tiny leaflet are caused neither
by its content nor by the psychological tension which it
creates among the people of the day. The actual event of
this letter consists oddly enough not in the letter itself,
but in its title—*Mundus Novus*—two words, four sylla-
bles, which revolutionize the conception of the cosmos as
had nothing before. Up to this hour Europe had consid-

ered that the greatest geographical event of the time was that India, the land of treasure and spice, had been reached within one decade by two different routes: by Vasco da Gama sailing eastward round Africa, and by Christopher Columbus travelling westward across the hitherto unexplored ocean. With amazement the world had admired the treasures which Vasco da Gama had brought back from the palaces of Calicut, and with curiosity listened to the tales of the many islands Christopher Columbus had found extending along the coast of what he considered to be China. What was more, according to his own ecstatic reports, he also had set foot on the great Khan's land, which Marco Polo had described. Thus the world seemed to have been encircled, and India, inaccessible for a thousand years, reached from both sides.

But there now appears this other sailor, the strange Albericus, with something much more surprising to tell. What he found on his voyage westward, so he says, was not India at all, but an entirely new unknown land, between Asia and Europe, and so an altogether new part of the world. Literally, Vesputius writes that these regions, which he had discovered in the service of the King of Portugal, might as well be called a new world—*"No-*

vum Mundum appellare licet"—and he is at great pains
to give reasons for his opinion. "For none of our ancestors
had any knowledge of the countries we saw, nor any idea
what they contained. Our knowledge goes far beyond
theirs. Most of them believed that no mainland existed
south of the equator, that there were only endless stretches
of sea which they called the Atlantic. And even those who
considered the existence of a continent possible were for
various reasons convinced that it must be uninhabitable.
My voyage has now proved this view erroneous and directly opposed to the truth, since I did find a continent
south of the equator, many parts of which are more popu-
lated by men and animals than are our Europe, Asia, and
Africa—and which, moreover, has a milder and pleasanter
climate than other continents known to us."

These few but conclusive words make of the *Mundus
Novus* a memorable document. They are, in fact—some
two hundred and seventy years before the official one—
the first Declaration of Independence of America. Columbus, up to the hour of his death blindly entangled in the
delusion that by landing in Guanahani and Cuba he had
set foot in India, has with this illusion actually decreased
the size of the cosmos for his contemporaries. Only Ves-

pucci, by destroying the hypothesis that this new country is India and insisting on its being a new continent, provides the new dimensions which have remained valid to this day. By so doing, he disperses the fog clouding the great discoverer's eye to his own feat; and even if he himself could not have anticipated the dimensions this continent was going to assume, nevertheless it was he who recognized at least the independence of its southern regions. In this sense Vespucci actually completes the discovery of America, for no invention, no discovery, becomes authentic through the man who makes it, but through the person recognizing its meaning and its true importance. If Columbus deserves the merit of the deed, so by these his words is due to Vespucci the historical credit of putting upon it the proper construction. As an interpreter of dreams, he made comprehensible what his forerunner had discovered as, so to speak, a somnambulist.

The surprise and joy which greet the announcement of this so far unknown Vesputius are colossal. It enters deep into the general feeling of the time—deeper even, and more lasting, than the discovery by the Genoese. The fact that a new route to India had been found, that now the countries described long ago by Marco Polo could also be reached by ship from Spain, had interested only a small circle of people directly concerned for commercial reasons—the merchants and tradesmen in Antwerp, Augsburg, and Venice, who are already busily calculating which route, that of Vasco da Gama eastward or of Columbus westward, is the cheaper for the shipment of pepper, cinnamon, and other spices. But the announcement of this Alberico to the effect that a new part of the world had been discovered in the middle of the ocean, stimulates the imagination of the great masses with irresistible power. Has he found the legendary island of Atlantis? The isles of bliss? The self-confidence of the time is peculiarly enhanced by the recognition that the world is larger and more full of surprises than even the wisest men of antiquity had conjectured, and that it is reserved for them, for their generation, to explore the final mysteries of the terrestrial globe. And it is not difficult to imagine the impatience with which the scholars, geographers, cosmographers, printers, and the vast mass of readers behind them wait for this unknown Albericus to fulfil his promise and tell more about his explorations and travels, which for the first time inform the world and humanity of the actual size of the globe.

Immortality from 32 Pages

These impatient people have not so very long to wait. Within two or three years—from a Florentine printer who wisely avoids mentioning his name, for reasons we shall understand later—there appears a thin booklet of sixteen leaves, in the Italian language. It is entitled *Lettera di Amerigo Vespucci delle isole nuovamente trovate in quattro suoi viaggi* ("A letter from Amerigo Vespucci, concerning the islands discovered on his four journeys"). At the end of this *opusculum* is the date: *"Data in Lisbona a di 4. septembre 1504. Servitore Amerigo Vespucci in Lisbona."*

From this title alone the world at last finds out something more about this mysterious man—first, that he is called Amerigo, and not Alberico; and Vespucci, instead of Vespucius. From the introduction, addressed to a great gentleman, more details of his life are clarified. Vespucci announces that he was born in Florence, and that he later moved on to Spain as a merchant *("per tractare mercantie")*. In this vocation he spent four years, during which he experienced the instability of fortune—"that perishable property, unevenly distributed, can one day carry man up to the heights, only to let him down on the next, thus depriving him of, so to speak, borrowed goods." But, he continues, as he had observed at the same time what dangers and inconveniences are connected with this pursuit of profit, he had decided to renounce the trade, and to set himself a higher and more glorious aim, namely, to see a part of the world and its wonders *("mi disposi d'andare a vedere parte del mondo e le sue maraviglie")*. For this, a good opportunity offered itself, since the King of Castile had equipped four ships with the object of discovering new land in the west, and he had been granted permission to accompany this fleet in order to help in the discovery *("per aiutare a discoprire")*. Vespucci, however, describes not only this voyage, but three others (among them that depicted in *Mundus Novus),* which are—the chronology being important—as follows:

The first, from May 10, 1497, to October 15, 1498, under the Spanish flag;

The second, from May 16, 1499, to September 8, 1500, again for the King of Castile;

The third *(Mundus Novus)* from May 10, 1501, to October 15, 1502, under the Portuguese flag;

The fourth from May 10, 1503, to June 18, 1504, again for the Portuguese.

With these four journeys the unknown merchant entered the ranks of the great navigators and discoverers of his day.

To whom this *Lettera*—this account of the four journeys—was sent is not mentioned in the first edition. Only in later editions are we told that it was addressed to the Gonfaloniere, the Governor of Florence, Piero Soderini. A convincing proof of this fact, however, is lacking even to this day—and the reader should be warned that he will soon find several such obscurities connected with Vespucci's literary production. But with the exception of a few polite phrases at the beginning, the form of the account is as light, amusing, and varied as that of the *Mundus Novus*. Apart from supplying fresh details about the "epicurean life" of these unknown people, he also describes battles, shipwrecks, and dramatic episodes with cannibals and giant snakes. Many animals and devices (the hammock, for example) are introduced to general knowledge for the first time by him. The geographers, the astronomers, and the merchants find valuable information; the scholars a number of theses which they can discuss and enlarge upon; and even the curiosity of the general public is satisfied. In conclusion, Vespucci once more announces his great, his real work devoted to these new worlds—a work which, as soon as he is able to settle down, he intends to write in his native town.

But this work never materialized, or—like Vespucci's diaries—it has not been preserved. Thus thirty-two pages (of which the third voyage is only a variation of the *Mundus Novus*) represent the entire literary output of Amerigo Vespucci—a tiny and not very solid piece of luggage for the journey into immortality. Never has any writing man become so famous on such meagre production; coincidence after coincidence, error after error, had to accumulate to raise it so high above its time as to make even us cognizant of the name that floats skyward with the starry banner.

The first coincidence, and incidentally the first error, soon came to the aid of these—in the higher sense—insignificant thirty-two pages. As early as 1504 a shrewd Italian printer correctly sensed that the time was ripe for travelogues. The Venetian Albertino Vercellese is the first to collect and make a small volume of all travel reports coming his way. This *Libretta de tutta la navigazione de Re de Spagna e terreni novamente trovati,* which includes the travel accounts concerning Cadamosto, Vasco da

Immortality from 32 Pages

Gama, and the first voyage of Columbus, has such an enormous sale that in 1507 a printer in Vicenza decides to publish a larger anthology (126 pages), under the direction of Zorzo and Montalboddo, containing the Portuguese expeditions of Cadamosto, Vasco da Gama, Cabral, the first three voyages of Columbus, and the *Mundus Novus* of Vespucci. He seems fated to find no better title for it than *Mondo novo e paesi nuovamente retrovati da Alberico Vesputio florentino* ("New world and countries newly discovered by Alberico Vespucci, Florentine"). With this there now begins the great comedy of errors, for this title has a dangerously ambiguous meaning. It suggests that the new countries were not only called a "New world" by Vespucci, but that they were also discovered by him. Anyone casting a fleeting glance at the title-page must inevitably be misled. And this book, printed over and over again, passes through thousands of hands, spreading with dangerous rapidity the false report that Vespucci was the first discoverer of these new countries. This ridiculous little accident of the innocent printer in Vicenza—that of placing Vespucci's name instead of Columbus's on the title-page of his anthology—transfers to the equally innocent Vespucci a fame of which he has no idea, and makes him, without his knowledge or desire, into the usurper of another's achievement.

This one error, of course, would not alone have been sufficient to cause the tremendous impression which lasted through the centuries; it was but the first act, or rather the prelude, to this comedy of errors. One knot of freak chance after another has to be tied before this deceptive web can be completed. Oddly enough, it is only now—after Vespucci has .brought to an end the whole literary achievement of his life with his miserable thirty-two pages—that his rise to immortality really begins: perhaps the most grotesque rise the history of fame has ever known. And it begins in a totally different part of the world, in a spot Vespucci has never set eyes on, and of whose existence the seafaring merchant in Seville probably never had the vaguest idea—in the little town of Saint-Dié.

4

A World Is Named

THERE is no need for anyone to feel embarrassed if he has never heard of the little town of Saint-Dié. Even the scholars took more than two centuries to discover the whereabouts of this *"Sancti Deodati oppidum,"* which had such a decisive influence on the naming of America. Hidden away in the shadows of the Vosges, and belonging to the long-vanished Duchy of Lorraine, this little place possessed nothing with which to attract the eyes of the world. Though the then reigning René II bears—as did his famous ancestor "le bon roi René"—the title of King of Jerusalem and Sicily and Count of Provence, he is in reality nothing but the duke of this small section of

Amerigo

Lorraine, which he governs honourably, with particular affection for the arts and sciences. Strangely enough (history loves the game of minor analogies), this small town has already been responsible for a book which had influence on the discovery of America. For it was just here that the Bishop d'Ailly wrote the work *Imago Mundi* which, together with Toscanelli's letter, supplied Columbus with the final impetus to sail in search of India by the western route. Up to his death the admiral always had with him this book as guide, and his own copy, preserved to this day, reveals innumerable marginal notes in his hand. Thus a certain pre-Columbian connexion between America and Saint-Dié cannot be denied. But it is only under the Duke René that there occurs the strange incident—or error—to which America owes its name for all time. Under the protection and probably also with the material aid of René II, a few humanists assemble in this tiny Saint-Dié and form a confraternity that calls itself Gymnasium Vosgianum, whose aim is both to teach and to spread knowledge by the printing of important books. In this miniature academy, laymen and men of the Church unite for cultural co-operation. But it is most probable these learned discussions would never have been heard of had not a printer by the name of Gauthier Lud decided, about 1507, to set up a press there and to print books. Actually, the place was well chosen, for in this little academy Gauthier Lud had at hand the right kind of men as editors, translators, proofreaders, and illustrators. In addition Strasbourg, with its university, is not far away. And since the generous duke, as protector, lends his support, an even larger work can be risked in this small secluded town, far from the world.

But what work? As the years pass and new discoveries enlarge the knowledge of the world, the curiosity of the time is directed toward geography. So far, in the geographic field only one classic book was known, the *Cosmographia* of Ptolemy; a work which, with its maps and explanations, had for a hundred years been considered by the scholars of Europe as unsurpassable and complete. Since 1475 it had been accessible to all educated people by reason of its having been translated into Latin, and as a general code of geography it had become indispensable; for what Ptolemy said and presented in his maps was regarded as fact simply through the authority of his name. But during the last twenty-five years the knowledge of the cosmos had been extended further than it had hitherto in centuries; and he who for a thousand years had been considered as knowing more than all cosmographers and geographers suddenly appeared to be lacking in his knowledge of the world and outclassed by a few daring seafarers and adventurers. So anyone wanting to republish the *Cosmographia* at that time had to correct and complete it; he had to insert into the old maps the new coast and islands which had been discovered in the west. Experience must rectify tradition; a modest correction must lend new belief to the respect for the classic work if in the future Ptolemy is to be considered omniscient and his book irrefutable. Prior to Gauthier Lud, no one had taken up the idea of supplementing the incomplete book. It is a responsible task, but one, incidentally, rich in prospects, and therefore the proper and obvious one for a group of people gathered together for co-operative work.

Gauthier Lud—not just a simple printer, but chaplain and secretary to the duke, and an erudite and even well-to-do man—inspects the little group and has to admit that he could not have been more fortunate. For the drawing and etching of maps there is an excellent young mathe-

A World Is Named

matician and geographer by the name of Martin Waldseemüller, who, according to the custom of the time so
far as learned books are concerned, has his name latinized
to Hylacomylus. Twenty-seven years old, a student of
Breisgau University, he combines the freshness and audacity of youth with a good intelligence and an eminent
talent for drawing, which for decades is to secure for his
maps a precedence in the history of cartography. There
is also present a young poet, Mathias Ringmann, who is
to call himself Philesius, and who is well fitted to introduce a work with a poetic epistle and to polish with taste
the Latin text. Nor is the perfect translator absent. He is
found in Jean Basin, who as a good humanist is not only
well versed in the ancient but also in the modern languages. With such a learned guild the revision of the
famous work can be approached without fear or hesita-
tion. But where is the detailed material for the presentation of these newly discovered zones to be found? Was
not this Vesputius one of the first to indicate this "new
world"? It was apparently Mathias Ringmann (who had
already published the *Mundus Novus* under the title of
De Ora Antarctica in Strasbourg in 1505) who suggested

that the Italian *Lettera,* still unknown in Germany, be translated into Latin and added to the work of Ptolemy as the natural supplement.

This by itself would have been a thoroughly honest and worthy undertaking, but the vanity of the publisher plays Vespucci a nasty trick, and thereby ties the second knot which the future is to use to twist the rope on the neck of the innocent man. Instead of stating truthfully that they translated the *Lettera* (Vespucci's report on his four journeys) from the original—that is, from the Italian into Latin—the humanists of Saint-Dié invent a romantic story, partly to attract more attention to their publication and partly in the eyes of the world to pay special tribute to their protector, Duke René. They trick the public into believing that Americus Vesputius, this famous geographer and discoverer of these new worlds, was a particular friend and admirer of their Duke, and that he had addressed this *Lettera* to him in Lorraine, pretending that this edition represented the first publication. What homage to their prince! With the exception of the King of Spain, so it is made to appear, the duke is the only man to whom the great scholar of his time, this world-famous man, sends an account of his journeys. With the idea of supporting this ingenious story, the dedication to the Italian *"Magnificenza"* is changed to the *"illustrissimus rex Renatus";* and, moreover, in order to conceal as thoroughly as possible the fact that it is but a question of a simple translation from an already printed Italian original, a note is added explaining that Vespucci had originally composed the work in French, and that it had then been translated by the *"insignis poeta"* Joannes Basinus (Jean Basin) from the French, *"ex gallico,"* into an elegant Latin, *"qua pollet elegancia latine interpretavit."* At closer inspection, this ambitious fraud proves rather transparent, for the *"insignis poeta"* has worked much too carelessly to obliterate all the traces pointing to the Italian origin. He calmly allows Vespucci to refer to facts which could have meant something only to Medici or Soderini, but certainly not to King René of Lorraine—that, for instance, they both studied together in Florence under his uncle Antonio Vespucci. Again, he allows him to speak of Dante as *"poeta nostro,"* which of course was conceivable only as coming from one Italian to another. But it is centuries before this swindle—of which Vespucci is as innocent as in everything else—is brought to light. And in hundreds of works (until very recently) these four

travel accounts are actually considered to have been addressed to the Duke of Lorraine. All Vespucci's glory and
his disgrace are based on this book printed in a corner of
the Vosges without his knowledge.

But all this is a background made up of machinations
and business practices of which the age is quite ignorant.
The booksellers, the scholars, the princes, and the merchants merely notice the appearance one day (April 15,
1507) at the Book Fair of a work of 52 pages, entitled
*Cosmographiæ Introductio. Cum quibusdam geometriæ
ac astronomiæ principiis ad eam rem necessariis. Insuper
quatuor Americi Vespucii navigationes. Universalis cosmographiæ descriptio tam in solido quam plano eis etiam
insertis quæ in Ptolemeo ignota a nuperis reperta sunt.
(Introduction to Cosmography, with the necessary funda-
mental principles of geometry and astronomy. Included
are the four journeys of Amerigo Vespucci; and furthermore a description* [map] *of the Universe both flat and
spherical of all those parts which were unknown to Ptolemy, and recently discovered.)* Anyone opening this small
volume must first of all bear with the poetic vanity of the

publishers, who make an effort to exhibit their poetic talent in the form of a short dedicatory poem in Latin by Mathias Ringmann to the Emperor Maximilian, and a preface by Waldseemüller-Hylacomylus to the Emperor, at whose feet he lays the volume. Only after the two humanists have indulged their vanity does Ptolemy's text begin. Then, after a brief announcement, there follows the description of Vespucci's journeys. With this publication in Saint-Dié the name of Amerigo Vespucci has again risen enormously, though of course it has not yet reached its peak. In the Italian anthology *Paesi nuovamente retrovati* his name had still been mentioned on the title-page in a somewhat ambiguous way as the discoverer of the "New World," and in the text his journeys were mentioned in one breath with those of Columbus and other explorers. In the *Cosmographiæ Introductio* the name of Columbus no longer appears—possibly an accident caused by the ignorance of the Vosgian humanists, but a fateful accident; for by it all light, all merit, of the discovery falls bright and dazzling on Vespucci alone. In the second chapter, in the description of the world known already to Ptolemy, it is said that though it had been extended in size by others, it was only now brought to the knowledge of humanity by Americo Vesputio—*"nuper vero ab Americo Vesputio latius illustratam."* In the fifth chapter he is explicitly acknowledged as the discoverer of these new zones—*"et maxima pars Terræ semper incognitæ nuper ab Americo Vesputio repertæ."* And in the seventh chapter there is suddenly posed the question whose consequences are to be decisive for centuries to come. When Waldseemüller mentions the fourth part of the world—*"quarta orbis pars"*—he adds as his own personal suggestion, *"quam quia Americus iuvenil Amerigen quasi Americi terram, sive Americam nuncupare licet"*—"which, since Americus found it, could from now on be called the Earth of Americus, or America."

These three lines are America's actual certificate of baptism. On this quarto sheet its name is for the first time formed in letters and multiplied in print. If one considers the twelfth of October 1492, the day Columbus spied the first shimmer off the coast of Guanahani from the deck of the *Santa Maria,* as the real birthday of the new continent, then one must call this twenty-fifth of April 1507, when the *Cosmographiæ Introductio* left the printing-press, its christening day. Though it is only a suggestion made by the so far nameless twenty-seven-

year-old humanist in the remote little town, he himself
is so enchanted by his own suggestion that he repeats it
a second time, and more forcefully. In the ninth chapter
Waldseemüller enlarges on his idea in a special paragraph. "Today," he writes, "these parts of the world
[Europe, Africa, and Asia] are already completely explored, and a fourth continent discovered by Amerigo
Vespucci. And as Europe and Asia have received fem-
inine names, I see no reason why this new region should
not be called Amerige, the land of Amerigo, or America,
after the sagacious man who discovered it." Or, to quote
his own Latin words:

*"Nunc vero et hae partes sunt latius lustratæ et alia
quarta pars Americum Vesputium (ut in sequentibus
andietur) inventa est, quam non video cur quis iure vetet
ab Americo inventore sagacis ingenii viro Amerigem
quasi Americi terram sive Americam dicendam; cum et
Europa et Asia a mulieribus sua sortita sunt nomina."*

At the same time Waldseemüller has the word "America" printed in the margin, and even writes it on the map
of the world which accompanies the work. From this
hour on, and without any knowledge of it himself, the
mortal Amerigo Vespucci wears over his head the aura

of immortality. At this moment America is called America for the first time, and will retain this name for ever.

"But that's absolutely ridiculous!" some reader may ex-
claim indignantly. "How can this twenty-seven-year-old
provincial geographer have the audacity to name an entire huge continent after a man who never discovered
America, and on no better evidence than a rather dubious
report of thirty-two pages?" But such indignation is anach-
ronistic, for it fails to consider the situation from the
historical point of view, but judges it rather through the
eyes of the present time. When pronouncing the word
"America," the people of our day err involuntarily by
thinking in terms of the magnificent continent reaching from Alaska to Patagonia. In the year 1507, neither
the benevolent Waldseemüller nor any other mortal
had the remotest idea of the size of the newly discovered "Mundus Novus." And one glance at the map
at the beginning of the sixteenth century will suffice
to give some idea what the cosmography of the time
imagined the "Mundus Novus" to be. In the midst of the
dark soup of the world ocean swim a few awkward-
looking chunks of land, only the edges of which have

been nibbled at by the curiosity of the explorers. The tiny piece of North America, where Cabot and Cortereal landed, is still stuck onto Asia, so that in the imagination of the time Boston was only a few hours from Peking. Florida, lying off Cuba and Haiti, is a large island; and in the place of the isthmus of Panama, connecting North and South America, there is a great sea. Finally, south of here, this new unknown land (the Brazil of today), a huge island, a kind of Australia, is marked in. On the maps it is called Terra Sancta Crucis, or Mundus Novus, or Terra dos Papagaios—all clumsy, inconvenient names for a new country. And as Vespucci is the first—not to discover these coasts, which Waldseemüller does not know —but to describe and introduce them to Europe, Waldseemüller only follows a general custom when he suggests Amerigo's name. Bermuda is named after Juan Bermudez, Tasmania after Tasman, Fernando Po after Fernando Po, so why should not this new country be named . after its first advertiser? It is a friendly gesture of a scholar's gratitude toward a man who was the first—and this is Vespucci's historical merit—to support the theory that America was not part of Asia, but represented a new continent—*"quartum pars mundi."* That with this well-

meant gesture he was assigning to Vespucci not Terra
Sancta Crucis, which he presumed to be an island, but an
entire continent, from Labrador to Patagonia, and by so
doing robbing Columbus, the real discoverer of this continent, of his achievement—of all this the friendly Waldseemüller had not the vaguest notion. And how, after all,
could he have suspected it when Columbus himself had
no idea—Columbus, who instead passionately and ex-
citedly insists that Cuba is China and Haiti Japan? With
this christening of America a new thread of error is drawn
into the already somewhat tangled skein; anyone touching the problem of Vespucci, however good his intentions,
has so far always introduced a fresh knot, and by so
doing made the whole net all the more difficult to
disentangle.

Thus it is thanks solely to a misunderstanding that
America is called America. Actually, the misunderstanding is twofold; for had the *"insignis poeta,"* Jean Basin,
chosen to translate the name Amerigo into Latin, Albericus, as others had, then New York and Washington
today would lie not in America but in Alberica. But now
the letters of this name have finally been cast, the letters

A World Is Named

formed into a word, and so it passes from book to book, from mouth to mouth, irrevocable and unforgettable. It exists, it lives, this new word, and not only by the accidental suggestion of Waldseemüller, not by logic or by chance, by right or wrong, but by its inherent phonetic power. America—the word begins and ends with the fullest-sounding vowel in our language. It is good for the cry of enthusiasm, clear for the memory—a strong, full, masculine word, fitting for a young country and a strong nation striving for development. The insignificant little geographer unconsciously created something of meaning with his historical mistake when he gave this world rising out of the dark this brother name to Asia, Europe, and Africa.

It is a conquering word; it has power; impetuously it thrusts aside all other names. It is only a few years since the *Cosmographiæ Introductio* has appeared, and it has already blotted out such names as "Terra dos Papagaios," "Isla de Santa Cruz," "Brazzil," and "Indias Occidentales" in the books and maps. A conquering word, every year it attracts more and more attention, a thousand times more than the good Martin Waldseemüller had ever dreamt of. In 1507 "America" still stands for no more than the Brazilian north coast; and the south, with the Argentine, is still known as "Brasilia Inferior." Had Amerigo's name been given only to this one coast which Vespucci was the first to describe, or even to the whole of Brazil, nobody would have accused him of shady dealings. However, it was a matter of but a few years before the name of America had dragged to itself the whole of the Brazilian coast, the Argentine, and Chile—parts of the world which the Florentine had never set eyes on. Anything discovered south of the equator, no matter in what direction, becomes Vespucci's land. Finally, about fifteen years after the appearance of Waldseemüller's book, the whole of South America is already known as America. All the great cartographers—including Simon Grynæus in his *Orbis Novus,* and Sebastian Münster in his maps of the world—have bowed before the will of the young schoolmaster of Saint-Dié. But the triumph is still incomplete. The great comedy of errors has not yet come to an end. On the maps, North America is still detached from South America, as though it were another world; sometimes, thanks to the ignorance of the age, it forms part of Asia and at other times is separated from Amerigo's continent by an imaginary strait. Finally, however, science does grasp the fact that this con-

tinent is a unit, from one polar sea to the other, and that
they should be linked together under one single name.
And it is then that this proud, unconquerable word, this
bastard of an error and a truth, rises up powerfully to
seize the immortal victim. As early as 1515 Johann
Schöner, the Nürnberg geographer, in a small pamphlet,
America sive Amerigem, which accompanied his globe,
had publicly proclaimed it as *"Novus Mundus et quarta
orbis pars,"* the fourth part of the world. And in 1538
Mercator, the king of geographers, draws the whole continent as a unit into his map of the world, writing the
name of America over both parts: A M E over the north
and R I C A over the south. And from this day no other
name is legitimate. In thirty years Vespucci has conquered
a quarter of the world for himself and his posthumous
fame.

This baptism without the knowledge or consent of the
father is an episode without parallel in the history of
earthly renown. With two words—"Mundus Novus"—a
man made himself famous; with three lines from an insignificant geographer he found immortality. Hardly ever
have error and chance been responsible for such an auda-

cious comedy. But in this comedy of errors history, just as magnificent in tragedy as inventive in farce, has contrived a peculiarly subtle point. Waldseemüller's suggestion has hardly reached the public before it is immediately received with enthusiasm. One edition follows another; all new geographical works accept the name "America"—after its "inventor," Amerigo Vespucci—and the cartographers are particularly ready to take note of the word. The name America is to be found everywhere—on every globe and map, in every book and letter—with one exception: a single map, a map appearing in 1513, and thus six years after Waldseemüller's original one bearing the name America. But who is this obstinate geographer indignantly rebelling against the new name? Ludicrously enough, it is none other than the very man who invented this name—Waldseemüller himself! Had he grown frightened, like the sorcerer's apprentice in Goethe's poem, who with one word transformed the dry broom into a wild and raging creature, and then did not know the other word to check the invoked spirit? Had he been warned by someone, possibly Vespucci himself, that he had wronged Columbus by conferring his achievement upon its interpreter? No one knows. No one will ever

A World Is Named

know why Waldseemüller himself wished to deprive the new continent of the name America, which he invented. In any case, it is too late for any correction. Truth rarely catches up with legend: a word once pronounced to the world draws power from this world, and continues to live free and independent of him who gave it birth. In vain does the insignificant little man, who was the first to pronounce it, try shamefully to suppress and keep secret the word America—for it is already floating in the air, leaping from letter to letter, from book to book, mouth to mouth; flying through space and time, irresistible and immortal, for it represents at once reality and idea.

5

The Great Dispute Begins

1512. Accompanied by a few people, a coffin is being borne from a church in Seville to the cemetery. It is neither a remarkable nor a pompous funeral, not that of a rich man or of a nobleman. Some official of the King, the Pilot Major of the Casa de Contratación, a certain Despuchy or Vespuche, is being laid to rest. No one in the foreign town has any idea it is the very man whose name will be borne by a fourth part of the world; nor do the historians or the chroniclers so much as mention this unimportant passing. Even thirty years later people are to read in the history books that Amerigo Vespucci died in 1534 in the Azores. Entirely unnoticed, the godfather

The Great Dispute Begins

of America fades out, as quietly as in 1506 the Adelantado, the great admiral of the New India, Cristoforo Colombo, was laid to rest in Valladolid, with neither king nor duke accompanying his coffin, and no contemporary historian considering his death important enough to be announced to the world.

Two forgotten graves in Seville and Valladolid. Two men who often met in their lives, without avoiding or hating each other; two men inspired by the same spirit of creative curiosity, who had been helping each other honestly and cordially on their ways. But over their graves the bitter dispute begins. Neither of them could have had any notion that the fame of the one would conflict with that of the other; that error, ignorance, curiosity, and self-righteousness would ever seek to create between the two great seafarers a rivalry which in real life never existed. But they themselves are to hear as little of the quarrel and uproar as of the wind which with unintelligible words whispers over their tombs.

The one who succumbs in this grotesque struggle of one fame against another is at first Columbus. He has died a defeated, humiliated, and half-forgotten man. A man of single purpose, single achievement, he had his immortal moment when his idea was realized in action: on the day when his *Santa Maria* landed on the coast at Guanahani, when the so far unconquerable Atlantic had been crossed for the first time. Up to this hour the great Genoese had been looked upon by the world as a fool, a fantastic person, a confused and unrealistic dreamer. And from this moment he is once more considered as such, for he cannot free himself from the illusion which egged him on. When he announces that "he has set foot on the richest kingdoms of the world"; when he promises gold, pearls, and spices from "India," he is still believed. A powerful fleet is equipped; fifteen hundred men fight for the honour of travelling with it to El Dorado and Ophir, which he insists on having seen with his own eyes; and the Queen presents him with letters wrapped in silk for the "great Chan" in Quinsay. Then he returns from this long voyage, and all he brings home is a few hundred half-starved slaves whom the pious Queen refuses to sell. A few hundred slaves and the old illusion that he had been in China and Japan, an illusion which becomes increasingly confused and all the more fantastic the less it is verified. In Cuba he assembles his men and, under threat of corporal punishment, makes them solemnly

The Great Dispute Begins

swear before an *escribano,* a notary, that Cuba is not an island, but the Chinese mainland. The helpless seamen shrug their shoulders over the fool, and sign, without taking him seriously; and one of them, Juan de Cosa, ignoring the oath, calmly draws Cuba as an island on his map. Unperturbed, however, Columbus continues to write to the Queen that "only a channel separated them from the Golden Chersonese of Ptolemy" (the Malay Peninsula), and that "it was no further from Panama to the Ganges than from Pisa to Genoa." At first, the court continues to smile; but it is not long before people begin to grow discontented. The expeditions are very costly, and what, after all, do they bring home? Weakly, starved slaves instead of the promised gold; and diseases instead of spices. The islands, with whose administration the Crown had entrusted him, become ghastly slaughter-houses and gruesome fields of carnage. In Haiti and the neighbouring islands a million natives perish within one decade; the immigrants grow impoverished, and rebel; terrible news of inhuman cruelties arrive with every letter, and of the disappointed colonists fleeing this "earthly paradise." It is soon understood in Spain that this fantastic man knows only how to dream, not to rule. The first thing the new governor, Bobadilla, sees from his ship is gallows from which corpses of his countrymen are swaying in the wind. The Columbus brothers have to be brought home in chains, and even when freedom, honour, and title are restored to Columbus, his prestige in Spain is utterly destroyed. No longer is his ship welcomed with great expectations on landing. When he attempts to appear at court he is avoided, and the old man, the discoverer of America, has to beseech permission to use a mule on the road. He continues, however, to make more and more fantastic promises; he pledges the Queen that on his next voyage he will discover "the Paradise," and the Pope that he intends to "liberate Jerusalem" by a crusade on the new and shorter route. In his *Book of Prophecies* he announces to sinful humanity that in a hundred and fifty years the world will come to an end. Finally, no one listens any more to the *"fallador"* (chatterbox) and his *"imaginações com su Ilha Cipangu"* (his fantasies concerning the island of Zipangu). The merchants who lost money through him, the scholars who despise his geographical nonsense, the colonists whom he disappointed with his great promises, and the officials who begrudge him his high position —all begin to form a closed front against the "Admiral of

The Great Dispute Begins

Mosquitoland." The old man is more and more edged aside, and he himself confesses ruefully: "I told them I had set foot on the richest kingdoms. I talked of gold, pearls, jewels, and spices—and because these things did not immediately appear, I fell into disgrace." About the year 1500 Christopher Columbus is finished in Spain, and at the time of his death he is almost forgotten.

Even the succeeding decades barely remember him, for it is a fast-moving age. Every year produces new heroic deeds, new discoveries, new names, new triumphs; and in such times yesterday's achievements are quickly forgotten. Vasco da Gama and Cabral return from India, bringing with them not naked slaves and vague promises, but precious objects from the East. King Manuel—"el Fortunado"—becomes the wealthiest monarch in Europe, thanks to this booty from Calicut and the Moluccas. Brazil is discovered; the Pacific Ocean is seen for the first time by Núñez de Balboa from the heights of Panama; Cortés conquers Mexico; Pizarro, Peru; and at last real gold flows into the coffers of the treasure houses. Magellan sails round America on his flagship *Victoria,* which, after a voyage of three years, returns to Seville, having circumnavigated the globe—the most magnificent feat of

seamanship of all time. In 1545 the silver mines of Potosí
are opened up, and every year the fleets return heavily
laden to Europe. In half a century all oceans have been
crossed; all, or almost all, countries of the terrestrial sphere
circumnavigated; so it can be imagined how little the
single man and his deed count in this Homeric epic. The
books describing his life and explaining his lonely foresight have not yet appeared. It is not long before the voyage of Columbus is considered but one in the glorious host
of the new Argonauts. And as he has delivered the least
tangible and valuable spoils, he is underestimated and forgotten by his age which, like all ages, thinks only in its
own terms and not in those of history.

Meanwhile, Amerigo Vespucci's fame begins to spread.
When everyone else was deluded and beguiled into believing that India had been discovered in the west, he recognized the truth: that this was a Novus Mundus, a new
world, another continent. He had never told anything but
the truth, never made promises of gold and jewels, but
announced modestly that, though the natives asserted they
had found gold in these lands, he preferred to remain, like
Saint Thomas, wary in his faith. Time would tell. Nor,

The Great Dispute Begins

like all the others, had he started out in search of gold and riches, but for the idealistic pleasure of discovery. Unlike the other criminal conquistadors, he refrained from torturing peoples and destroying countries. As a humanist and a learned man, he studied their customs and needs without praise or criticism. As a wise pupil of Ptolemy and the great philosophers, he observed the stars and their movements, and explored the oceans and countries for their marvels and mysteries. It was no mere chance that guided him, but uncompromising mathematical and astronomical science. Yes, indeed—declare the scholars—he is one of them: *"Homo humanus,"* a humanist! He knows how to write; and he knows his Latin, the only language they hold proper for things of the spirit. He has saved the honour of science by serving it alone, in preference to profit and wealth. Every one of his contemporary historians, including Peter Martyr, Ramusio, and Oviedo, bows in homage while mentioning Vespucci's name. And since there are no more than a dozen scholars working to enlighten their generation, Vespucci is considered the greatest navigator of his time.

Thus in the final analysis Vespucci owes this prodigious prestige in the learned world to the accidental circum-

Amerigo

stance that his two thin and ambiguous pamphlets had appeared in Latin, the language of the scholars. In particular, it is the publication of the *Cosmographiæ Introductio* which provides them with overwhelming authority over the others. Only because he was the first to describe it is Vespucci unhesitatingly celebrated as the discoverer of this New World by the scholars, to whom the word means more than the deed. Schöner, the geographer, is the first to draw the dividing line, declaring that Columbus discovered only a few islands, while Vespucci found the New World. And within one decade, through repetition in speech and writing, it has already become an axiom that Vespucci was the discoverer of the new continent, and that it is only right that America is known as America.

This fallacious glory of Vespucci as discoverer of the New World shines bright and undimmed through the whole of the sixteenth century. Only once is a rather feeble protest uttered. It comes from a strange man, one Miguel Serveto, who later attained the tragic fame of being thrown on the pyre by Calvin in Geneva, as the first victim of a Protestant Inquisition. Servetus's character is an

The Great Dispute Begins

extraordinary one in the history of the human intellect: half-genius, half-fool, he is a dissatisfied, cavilling will-o'-the-wisp, who always feels obliged to present his opinion in the most violent manner in every field of science. But this actually unproductive man possesses a strange instinct for touching everywhere on important problems. In medicine he foresees, almost exactly, Harvey's theory of the circulation of the blood; in theology he puts his finger on Calvin's greatest weakness; in everything he is aided by a strange faculty of foresight, if not to solve problems, at least to bring them to light. In geography, too, he touches on the crucial problem. Outlawed by the Church, he flees to Lyon, where he practises as a physician under an assumed name, and publishes at the same time, in 1535, a new edition of Ptolemy which he furnishes with his own comments. To this publication are added the maps of Laurent Frisius's edition (1522) of Ptolemy, which, on Waldseemüller's suggestion, mark the southern part of the continent "America." But whereas in 1522 Ptolemy's publisher, Thomas Ancuparius, sings Vespucci's praises in his preface, without even mentioning Columbus, Servetus is the first to raise certain objections against the general overestimation of Vespucci and the suggested christening

of the new continent. After all, he writes, Vespucci started
out as a mere merchant *("ut merces suas comutaret")* and
"multo post Columbus," long after Columbus. It is still a
very cautious utterance, a whispered protest, so to speak.
Nor does it occur to Servetus to deprive Vespucci of his
fame as a discoverer; it is only an attempt on his part to
prevent Columbus from being entirely ignored. Thus, so
far, it is by no means a question of Columbus *or* Vespucci;
no dispute for priority has yet begun. What Servetus hints
at is only that people should recognize Vespucci *and* Columbus. And so it is that without the possession of con-
crete proofs, without more exact knowledge of the historical situation, but simply from his suspicious instinct of
sensing errors and tackling problems from a fresh angle,
Servetus is the first to indicate that all is not well with
Vespucci's fame—a fame which had been let loose on the
world with the violence of an avalanche.

Really decisive protests, of course, can come only from
someone who is not—like Servetus in Lyon—dependent
on books and uncertain reports, but who has access to
trustworthy knowledge of factual historical events. But
there is about to be heard a powerful voice destined to

rise against the exaggerated renown of Vespucci, a voice
to which Emperors and Kings shall be compelled to lis-
ten and whose word is to free millions of tormented people: the voice of the great Bishop Las Casas, who dis-
closed the abominations perpetrated by the conquistadors
against the natives with such overwhelming power that
even today his reports can be read with a palpitating
heart. Las Casas, who passed the age of ninety, has been
an eye-witness of the whole age of discovery; and thanks
to his love of truth and his priestlike impartiality, he was
an incorruptible witness. Even today his famous history
of America, *Historia general de las Indias,* which he began in 1559 in a Valladolid monastery in his eighty-fifth
year, can be considered the most solid foundation of historical writing of that epoch. Born in 1474, he had come
to Hispaniola (Haiti) in 1502 (thus still in Columbian
times), and—with the exception of a number of journeys
to Spain—had spent his whole life up to his seventy-third
year as a priest, and later as bishop, in the New World.
So no one was more entitled and better fitted to give a
suitable and authentic judgment concerning the happen-
ings during the epoch of discovery.

Returning to Spain from one of his journeys to the

Amerigo

"Nuevas Indias," Las Casas must have run across one of these maps or foreign books in which the new land was marked with the name "America." And, probably just as astonished as ourselves, he must have asked: "Why America?" The answer, that Amerigo Vespucci discovered it, must naturally have stirred his suspicion and anger. For if anyone was informed of the situation it was surely he. His own father had personally accompanied Columbus on his second journey, with the result that he himself could thus testify that Columbus, in his own words, was "the first to have opened the gates of this ocean, which for so many centuries had been locked." In which case, how could Vespucci boast of, or be lauded for, being the first discoverer of this world? It looks as though he then happened upon the current argument that Columbus had discovered only the islands lying to the east of America, the Antilles, and Vespucci the real mainland. And he might therefore rightly be considered the discoverer of the continent.

But now Las Casas, usually such a mild man, grows furious. If Vespucci really means this, he says, then he is a liar. None other than the admiral was the first to set foot on the mainland at Parias, on his second journey, in

The Great Dispute Begins

the year 1498. This, moreover, was testified to by the solemn oath of Alonso de Hojeda in the trial of the treasury *versus* the heirs of Columbus in the year 1516. Furthermore, not one of more than a hundred witnesses in the trial had dared dispute this fact. By rights, this country should be called "Columba." How, then, could Vespucci "usurp the honour and fame which belonged to the Adelantado, and claim the achievement for himself?" Where and when and with which expedition had he been on the mainland in advance of the admiral?

Las Casas now investigates Vespucci's report, as printed in the *Cosmographiæ Introductio,* in an attempt to impeach Vespucci's claim of priority. Whereupon there appears a new and grotesque turn in this comedy of errors, giving the already well-entangled ball a fresh push in quite a wrong direction. In the original Italian edition in which Vespucci's first journey of 1497 is described, it is mentioned that he landed in a place called "Lariab." Owing to a printing error or an intentional emendation, the Latin edition of Saint-Dié substitutes for this "Lariab" the word "Parias," thus giving the impression that Vespucci himself claimed to have been in Parias as early as 1497, and so on the mainland one year before Columbus.

Amerigo

Thus Las Casas is left with no doubt that Vespucci is a forger who, after the admiral's death, made good use of the opportunity to pose as the discoverer of the new continent "in foreign books," since in Spain they would have kept too strict an eye on him. Now Las Casas goes on to prove that in reality Vespucci sailed to America in 1499, and not in 1497, and that he prudently omitted the name of Hojeda. "What Amerigo has written," angrily exclaims the honest man, "to make himself famous by calmly usurping the discovery of the mainland" had been accomplished with evil intent, thus turning Vespucci into a swindler.

Actually, what causes Las Casas's excitement over the allegedly intentional fraud—the substitution of the word "Parias" for the original word "Lariab"—is but a printer's error in the Latin edition. But Las Casas, without meaning to, has touched on a sore spot, namely, that in all Vespucci's letters and reports there prevails a strange obscurity concerning the intentions and the actually achieved aims of his journeys. Vespucci is never clear about the names of the commanders of the fleet; his dates vary in the different editions; his degrees of longitude are incor-

rect. From the moment experts tried to establish the
historical foundations of his journeys, the suspicion arose
that for some reasons—with which we shall deal later—
the actual state of affairs had been intentionally rendered
obscure. And now for the first time we approach the real
Vespucci secret, which for centuries preoccupied the scholars of all nations: how much in the reports of his journeys
is truth, and how much fiction, or, to be more severe,
falsification?

This doubt concerns above all the first of the four journeys, that of May 10, 1497, which Las Casas had already
contested, and which at best could have secured for Vespucci a certain priority as the discoverer of the new continent. This journey is not mentioned in any historical
work; certain elements in it are doubtless borrowed from
the second voyage with Hojeda. Even the most fanatical
defenders of Vespucci could not legitimate a sea voyage
of his during this year, and had to content themselves
with hypotheses in order to offer it some semblance of
probability. To give in detail the proofs and counter-proofs
of these endless and sharply contradictory discussions of
the learned geographers would alone fill a book. Suffice it
to say that three-quarters of them reject this first journey

as imaginary, whereas the remainder of his *ex officio* defendants allow Vespucci to be the first discoverer at one time of Florida, at another of the Amazon. But since the immense prestige of Vespucci has been resting mainly on this first most dubious journey, it is obvious that this tower of Babel, built out of error, accident, and ignorant babbling, would begin to sway as soon as someone touched its foundations with a philological axe.

This decisive blow is dealt by Herrera in 1601 in his *Historia de las Indias Occidentales*. The Spanish historian did not have to go to any great trouble for his arguments, since he had access to the still-unpublished book of Las Casas; and so it is actually Las Casas who is inveighing against Vespucci. With Las Casas's arguments, Herrera explains and proves that the dates of the *Quatuor Navigationes* are incorrect, that Vespucci sailed in 1499 with Hojeda, and not in 1497; and he comes to the conclusion—without the accused's having a chance to put in a word—that Amerigo Vespucci had "cunningly and intentionally falsified his reports with the object of robbing Columbus of the honour of having been the discoverer of America."

The reverberations of this disclosure are tremendous.

The Great Dispute Begins

What's this?—the scholars start up in alarm—Vespucci not
the discoverer of America after all? The wise man, whose
discreet modesty we have admired so much, turning out
to be a liar, an impostor, a Mendez Pinto, a man incapable
of telling the truth about a voyage of discovery? What's
more, if he can lie about one journey, why should the
others be true? What a disgrace that the modern Ptolemy
should turn out to be nothing but a wicked Herostratus,
cunningly breaking his way into the Hall of Fame and
buying himself immortality with a villainous crime!
What a disgrace for the whole learned world that—taken
in as they were by his vainglorious chatter—it should have
given the new continent his name! Wasn't it about time
to correct this embarrassing mistake? Whereupon, quite
seriously, in 1627, Fray Pedro Simon suggests "the sup-
pression of all geographical works and maps containing
the name America."

The pendulum has swung back. It is all over for Vespucci, and once again in the seventeenth century the half-
forgotten name of Columbus mounts in all its glory.
As imposing as the new land, his figure appears again.
Of all feats, only his has remained, for the palaces of

Amerigo

Montezuma are plundered and in decay; the treasure houses of Peru empty; all deeds and misdeeds of the conquistadors forgotten—only America is reality, an adornment of the earth, a home for all the persecuted, the land of the future. What injustice has been done to this man in his lifetime, and in the century after him! Columbus becomes a hero; all that was underestimated in his life changes fast into overestimation; anything shady in his portrait is effaced; men are dumb concerning his bad administration, his religious crotchets—in a word, they idealize his life. All the troubles he suffered are dramatically exaggerated: how he was compelled to use force when his sailors mutinied, how he was brought home in chains by a mean villain, and how he takes refuge with his half-starved child in a Rabida monastery. Against the former meagre celebration of his achievement the recognition now, thanks to the eternal impulse to hero-worship, becomes almost too great.

But according to the ancient law in all dramas and melodramas, every heroic figure requires its counterpart—just as light demands shadow, God the Devil, Achilles Thersites, and the crazy dreamer Don Quixote the primitive, realistic Sancho Panza. In order to reveal genius, its counterpart—petty obstacles, the base powers of ignorance, envy, and betrayal—must be exposed. Thus the enemies of Columbus—Bobadilla, an honest, just, insignificant official; and the Cardinal Fonseca, an able, clear-headed mathematician—are revealed as malicious villains. But the real enemy has now fortunately been found in Amerigo Vespucci, and in opposition to the Columbus legend there now arises that of Vespucci. There lives in Seville, so the people's story goes, a poisonous toad, swollen with envy, a small merchant whose desire it is to be taken for a scholar and an explorer. But he is too much of a coward ever to venture to sea. Grinding his teeth, he watches from the security of his home the great Columbus being received with pomp and jubilation on his return. How steal his fame? If only he could claim it for himself! So while the noble admiral is being dragged home in chains, he cunningly scribbles away at material torn from foreign books of travel. And hardly is Columbus buried, and thus incapable of defending himself, when this hyena for fame sends wooing letters and reports to all the world's potentates, claiming that he is the first, the real world-discoverer —at the same time taking good care to have them printed abroad, in Latin. He pleads with and begs unsuspecting scholars in some remote corner of the world, so the story goes on, to call the new continent America, after him. He sneaks up to Columbus's arch-enemy, his brother in envy, the Bishop Fonseca, and cunningly persuades him to appoint him—the insignificant clerk, totally ignorant of seamanship—*piloto mayor,* to the directorate of the Casa de Contratación, with the sole purpose of laying his hands on the maps. By so doing (for such are the things actually ascribed to Vespucci), he is at last provided with the possibility of the great betrayal: the *piloto mayor,* in charge of map-drawing and free from control, can cause all maps and globes everywhere to have the new land marked with his own infamous name—America, America, America! Thus the dead man, who, living, had been thrown into chains, is once more robbed and cheated by the genius for betrayal. It is not his name, but that of the thief, which now adorns the new continent.

Such is the picture of Vespucci during the seventeenth century—defamer, swindler, liar. The eagle who once surveyed the world with defiant eyes has suddenly turned into a disgusting, burrowing mole, a robber and desecrator of the dead. It is a thoroughly unjust picture, but it eats into the age. For decades, even centuries, Vespucci's name suffocates in filth. Both Bayle and Voltaire give him a kick in his grave, and the school books tell the children the story of his fraudulent acquisition of fame. Finally, three hundred years later (1856), even such a wise and considerate man as Ralph Waldo Emerson, still under the spell of this legend, is capable of writing:

"Strange that broad America must wear the name of a thief. Amerigo Vespucci, the pickle-dealer at Seville, whose highest naval rank was boatswain's mate in an expedition that never sailed, managed in this lying world to supplant Columbus and baptize half the earth with his own dishonest name."

6

The Documents
Play Their Part

I<small>N THE</small> seventeenth century Amerigo Vespucci is done for. The dispute over his name and over his achievement, or the contrary, seems to have ended for good. He is dethroned, found guilty of swindling, and—if America were not destined to bear his name—condemned to oblivion. But there is a new century beginning, one no longer willing to put its faith in mere gossip and rumours handed down by contemporaries of that time. The writing of history develops from mere chronicling to a critical science which makes it its business to investigate all facts, to examine all evidence. Documents are unearthed

The Documents Play Their Part

from all archives, then studied and collated. Thus it is inevitable for the old and apparently long since settled case of Columbus *versus* Vespucci to be resumed once more.

The beginning is made by his countrymen. They do not want to admit that the name of this Florentine, whose fame has made his native town renowned the world over, has been nailed to the pillory. So they are the first to demand a thorough and impartial revision. In 1745 the Abbot Angelo Maria Randini publishes the first biography of the Florentine navigator, *Vita e lettere di Amerigo Vespucci*. Francesco Bartolozzi, managing to bring to light a number of documents, follows in 1789 with new *Ricerche istorico-critiche,* and the results seem to the Florentines so encouraging for rehabilitation of their countryman that the Padre Stanislao Canovai utters a solemn and laudatory oration in favour of the slandered *"celebro navigator,"* an *Elogio d'Amerigo Vespucci*. At the same time a search is begun in the Spanish and Portuguese archives. A great deal of documentary dust is stirred up, but the greater the stir, the darker it grows.

The Portuguese archives are the less productive. There is not so much as a word about one of the two expeditions

Amerigo

Vespucci is supposed to have accompanied; no mention of his name in the account books; no trace of that *"zibaldone,"* his travel diary, which, according to himself, he had handed to the King of Portugal. Nothing—not a line, not a word. And immediately one of Vespucci's fiercest opponents declares this to be proof positive that Amerigo had simply invented these two journeys *"auspiciis et stipendio Portugallensium,"* under the promotion and with the financial aid of Portugal. But of course it is flimsy proof if after four hundred years no documents can be found concerning a single man who neither equipped nor commanded the expeditions. The greatest Portuguese, the pride of his nation, Luís de Camões, has been in Portuguese service for sixteen years, has been wounded fighting for his King, but not a single official line mentions this. He was arrested and incarcerated in India, but where are the documents relating these facts? Even concerning his journeys not a word can be found; and in a similar manner Pigafetta's diary on the still more memorable voyage of Magellan simply disappeared. But when the documentary evidence in Lisbon dealing with the most important period in Vespucci's life is found to be as good as naught, we should remember that it is no less than we know from

The Documents Play Their Part

archives of the African adventures of Cervantes, Dante's years of travel, or of Shakespeare's experience in the theatre. Moreover, Cervantes fought, Dante wandered from one country to another, and Shakespeare appeared hundreds of times on the stage. Even documents are not always valid proof, and still less the lack of documents.

The Florentine documents are of the greater import. In the public archives, Bandini and Bartolozzi find three letters from Vespucci to Lorenzo de' Medici. They are not originals, but later copies of a collection begun by a certain Vaglienti, who had copied in chronological sequence all reports, letters, and publications, dealing with voyages of discovery. One of these letters is written during the return from the third journey to Cape Verde—the first trip undertaken in the service of the King of Portugal. The second letter contains a more detailed description of this so-called third journey, and actually presents the substance of all that is later to be published in *Mundus Novus*—with the exception of certain rather suspicious literary trimmings. All this seems a splendid justification of Vespucci's love for the truth: at least his so-called third journey—the one that first made him famous through the

Amerigo

Mundus Novus—is now irrefutably proved, and he could already be congratulated as an innocent victim of baseless slander. But then appears a third letter to Lorenzo de' Medici, in which Vespucci—what a clumsy individual!—describes the first journey of 1497 as that of 1499, thus admitting precisely what his enemies accused him of, namely, that in the printed edition he had antedated his voyage by two years. According to this, his own report is incontestably substantiated—that he or someone else had fabricated two journeys out of one, and that the claim to have been the first to set foot on the American mainland had been both insolently as well as clumsily invented. And now Las Casas's grim suspicion cannot possibly be contradicted. Those desiring to rehabilitate Vespucci as a truthful man—his most fanatical defenders, and his countrymen in the *Raccolta Columbiana*—can find no other way out of this impasse but the last and most desperate: to declare this letter a forgery after the event.

Thus, with the aid of what was discovered in the Florentine archives, we are once more given a glimpse of the already known dual portrait of Vespucci—the man of shadowy outline; a man who, on the one hand in his private letters, reports honestly and modestly the true facts to his employer, Lorenzo de' Medici; and on the other, the Vespucci of the printed books, the man of great fame and cause of so much confusion, who untruthfully claims discoveries and voyages he has never made, and who with his boasting succeeds in getting an entire continent named after him. The longer the ball keeps on rolling through the years, the more error it gathers.

But, strangely enough, precisely the same divergence of facts is produced by the Spanish documents. From them we learn that Vespucci came to Seville in 1492, not as a great scholar, nor as a much-travelled seafarer, but as an insignificant employee, a "factor" in the firm of Juanoto Beraldi, a branch of the Medici bank in Florence, which dealt mainly in the equipment of ships and the financing of expeditions. This does not agree very well with the legend that Vespucci, as a leader of daring voyages of discovery, had sailed from Spain as early as 1497. What is still odder is that of this first journey, with which he was alleged to have forestalled Columbus, not the slightest trace can be found in all the documents; and so it is almost certain that, in the year 1497, instead of exploring the coasts of America, as is claimed in his *Quatuor Navi-*

gationes, he was in reality sitting busily engaged as a merchant in his office in Seville.

Once more, then, all accusations against Vespucci seem to be justified by documentary evidence. But, strange to relate, the same Spanish documents contain proofs speaking as convincingly for Vespucci's honesty as do others for his insolent boasting. There is a naturalization paper dated April 24, 1505, making Amerigo de Vespucci a Spanish citizen, "for the good services which he has rendered to the Crown, and which he is to continue to render." On March 22, 1508, there is the Casa de Contratación's promotion to *piloto mayor,* to the leader of the whole nautical service in Spain, ordering him "to instruct the helmsmen in the use of the instruments for measuring, the astrolabes and quadrants, and to examine their ability for combining theory sufficiently with practice." There is the royal command to manufacture a *"padrón real,"* a map of the world that will record definitely all newly discovered coasts, and that is to be continuously added to and corrected by him. Is it likely, now, that the Spanish Crown, which after all had the choice of the foremost navigators of the time, would appoint to such a responsible post one who, with his boasting and fictitious

stories, lacks all moral substance? Is it likely that the King
of Portugal would summon to his country just this man
to accompany two fleets to South America, if Vespucci
had not made a special name for himself as a nautical
expert? And is it not a proof of his honesty that Juanoto
Beraldi, in whose firm he has been working for years and
who ought therefore to be the best judge of his personal
reliability, should on his deathbed appoint just him as
the executor of his will and the liquidator of his business?
Once more we come upon the same contrast, that wherever we find a document dealing with Vespucci's life, he
is praised as an honest, reliable, knowledgeable man; and
yet the moment we are confronted with any of his writing in print, we find bragging, lies, and improbabilities.

But is it not possible to be an excellent seaman and at
the same time a teller of tall stories and an exaggerator?
Cannot a man be a good cartographer and incidentally
an envious character? Has not the telling of fabulous tales
been considered for centuries the vice of sailors, and envy
almost the professional disease of scholars? So none of
these documents is of any assistance to Vespucci faced
with the accusation of having treacherously conjured away
the discovery of America from the great admiral.

Amerigo

But now a voice rises from the grave to speak for Vespucci's honesty. And in the great trial of Columbus *versus* Vespucci, the man appearing as witness on Vespucci's behalf is just the one whom we would have least expected to testify for him—Cristoforo Colombo himself. On February 5, 1505, not long before his death, and so at the moment when the *Mundus Novus* must have been known in Spain for some time, the admiral, having already mentioned Vespucci as his friend in an earlier letter, addresses the following to his son Diego:

February 5, 1505

My dear Son:

Diego Mendez left here on Monday, the 3rd of this month. Since his departure I have talked with Amerigo Vespuchy, who is on his way to the Court, where he has been called to be consulted on several points connected with navigation. He has at all times shown the desire to be pleasant to me [*el siempre tuvo deseo de me hacer placer*]; he is an honest man [*mucho hombre de bien*]. As with many others, fortune has not been kind to him. His efforts have not brought him the reward he might by rights have expected. He is going there [to the Court] with the sincere desire to obtain something favourable for me [*que redonde a mi bien*], should the opportunity offer itself [*si a sus manos esta*]. From here I cannot advise him more specifically how to be of use to me, because I don't know what is expected of him; but he is decided to do all in his power on my behalf.

This letter provides one of the most surprising scenes in our comedy of errors. The two men whom the stupidity of three centuries imagined only as bitter rivals, fighting with bared teeth for the fame of having the new country called after them, were in reality cordial friends! Columbus, whose suspicious character brought him into conflict with almost all his contemporaries, praises Vespucci as a helper of long standing, and makes him his champion at the court! Thus neither of them—and this is undoubtedly a historical fact—had the remotest idea that ten generations of scholars and geographers would incite their ghosts against one another in a battle for the shadow of a name; that they were destined to become opponents in a comedy of errors—the one, the honest genius, robbed by the other, the wicked villain. Naturally, neither of them knew the word "America" round which the battle was to be fought; nor did Columbus guess that his islands, or Vespucci the coasts of Brazil, concealed behind them this gigantic continent. Men of the same craft, as little pampered by fortune as conscious of their prodigious fame, they understood one another better than have most of their biographers, who, with poor psychology, endowed them with a knowledge of their achievement quite impossible for them to have possessed at the time. Once again, as so often happens, truth destroys a myth.

The documents have begun to speak. But their very discovery and interpretation make the controversy over Vespucci flare up more violently than ever. Never before have thirty-two pages of text been scrutinized for their authenticity with such painstaking care from the psychological, geographical, historical, and typographical points of view as have these travel reports of Vespucci. But the result is that the warring geographers continue to defend their opposing opinions—their Yes and No, black and white, discoverer or fraud—with the same certainty and with proofs of allegedly equal infallibility. For the sake of amusement I shall merely mention here in passing what the various authorities maintained in their theories on Vespucci dur-

ing the nineteenth century. He made this first voyage
with Pinzón. He made it with Lepe. He sailed on this first
voyage with an unknown expedition. He did not make
it at all; it was a pure invention. On his first journey he
discovered Florida. He discovered nothing, for he never
embarked on the voyage. He was the first man to set eyes
on the Amazon. He saw this river only on his third voyage, because he had previously confused it with the Ori-
noco. He was the first to explore and name all the coasts
of Brazil down to the Strait of Magellan. He explored
only a few of them, and they had received their names
long before his arrival. He was a great navigator. No, he
never commanded either a ship or an expedition. He was
a great astronomer. Never—all he wrote about the constellations is nonsense. His dates are correct. His dates are
incorrect. He was an important pilot. He was nothing but
a "beef-contractor," and an uneducated ignoramus. His
assertions are reliable. He is a professional swindler, pres-
tidigitator, and liar. With the exception of Columbus, he
is the greatest discoverer and explorer of his time. He is
the pride of—no, a disgrace to—science.

All this is asserted in writing with the same vehemence
in his favour as in his disfavour, and is maintained and

substantiated with an incredible number of so-called proofs. And so the world is faced once more—just as it was three hundred years ago—with the same old question: "Who was Amerigo Vespucci? What did he do, and not do? Is there an answer? Can this great riddle be solved?"

7

Who Was Vespucci?

WE HAVE tried here to relate in chronological sequence the story of the great comedy of errors which developed round the life of Amerigo Vespucci over a period of three centuries, and which finally led to the calling of the new continent after his name. A man becomes famous without anyone's really knowing quite why. We can say, according to what we think, that he acquired it by right or not, by merit or by fraud. For Vespucci's fame is not so much fame as legend, because it came about not so much by his achievements as by the erroneous judgment of what he achieved.

The first error—the first act of our comedy—was the

connexion of his name with the book title *Paesi retrovati,*
by which the world was led to believe that Vespucci, and
not Columbus, had discovered these new countries. The
second error—the second act—was a typographical mistake, "Parias" for "Lariab" in the Latin edition, as a consequence of which it was maintained that not Columbus
but Vespucci was the first to set foot on the mainland of
America. The third error—the third act—was the mistake
of a small provincial geographer who on the strength of
Vespucci's thirty-two pages suggested that America should
be called after him. Up to the end of the third act Amerigo Vespucci is the hero, as in a real Rogue's Comedy.
As a hero without faults, as a heroic character, he holds
the stage. In the fourth act the suspicion concerning him
arises for the first time, and we no longer know whether
he is a hero or a swindler. The fifth act, the last, which
takes place in our century, must therefore still lead to an
unexpected climax in which the ingeniously tied knot can
be undone, and in the end all threads happily and definitely disentangled.

Fortunately history is an excellent dramatist, knowing
how to find a proper ending for its tragedies as well as
for its comedies. Since the fourth act we know this much:

Who Was Vespucci?

Vespucci has not discovered America, he was not the first to set foot on the mainland, and he never undertook this first journey, which for a long time made him the rival of Columbus. But while the scholars are squabbling on the stage as to how many other journeys described in his books Vespucci had made or not made, a man suddenly appears on the scene with the disconcerting suggestion that even these thirty-two pages, as we know them, had not been written by Vespucci; that these writings which had excited the world for so long were nothing but foreign, irresponsible, and wilful compilations, in which handwritten material of Vespucci's had been misused in the most insolent manner. This *deus ex machina,* Professor Magnaghi, thus sets the problem going anew by resolutely turning it upside down. While the others had taken for granted that Vespucci had at least written the books bearing his name, and doubted only whether he had actually undertaken the voyages described therein, Magnaghi contends that, though Vespucci had made journeys, it was very doubtful if he himself had written the books in their existing form. It was not he, therefore, who had boasted of fictitious achievements, but the mischief had been perpetrated and written under his name. So if we wish to do

Vespucci justice, it will be best for us to put aside his two famous printed pamphlets, the *Mundus Novus* and the *Quatuor Navigationes,* and proceed solely on the evidence of the three original letters which, without any real foundation, had been declared falsifications by his defenders.

The theory that Vespucci should not be made entirely responsible for the writings circulating under his name has at first a bewildering effect. For what, after all, remains of Vespucci's fame if even his books had not been written by him? But on closer inspection Magnaghi's theory proves to be not wholly novel. The suspicion that the swindle of the first journey has not been committed by Vespucci, but against him, is actually as old as the first accusation itself. It will be remembered that it was the Bishop Las Casas who was the first to accuse Vespucci of having forced his name on the new continent by the pretence of a voyage he had never undertaken. He accused Vespucci of a "great infamy," a "cunning fraud," and a "cruel injustice." But when his text is more closely examined, it will be found that through all his violent attacks there exists a certain *reservatio mentalis.* Though Las Casas reveals and attacks the fraud, he is always careful to write about a swindle which Vespucci "or those who published his *Quatuor Navigationes"* committed. He thus allows for the possibility of Vespucci's having acquired his false fame without his own participation. Similarly Humboldt—who, differing from professional theoreticians, is unready to take any printed book for gospel truth—utters a definite doubt about Vespucci's having become involved in the whole controversy, as did Pontius in the Credo. "Is it not possible," he asks, "that collectors of books on travel committed this fraud without Amerigo's knowledge, or is it perhaps only the consequence of a confused presentation and incorrect statements?"

Thus the key was already fashioned; Magnaghi had only used it to open the door onto a new prospect. So far, his interpretation seems to me the most logically convincing, because it is the only one seeming to solve in a completely natural manner all the contradictions that busied three centuries. From the beginning, it was psychologically improbable that the same man who wrote in a book about his fictitious journey of 1497 should at the same time change that date, in a handwritten letter, to the year 1499; or that he should have written of his journeys with different dates to two different people of this intimate circle in Florence, where letters after all were certain to pass from hand to hand. Furthermore, it seems improbable that a man living in Lisbon should have posted his reports to a petty prince in Lorraine, and that he should have had his opus printed in such an out-of-the-way little spot as Saint-Dié. Had he himself published his "works," or tried to do so, he would at least have taken the trouble to eliminate the most glaring mistakes before the book went to press. Is it likely, for example, that Vespucci himself would have reported to Lorenzo de' Medici in his *Mundus Novus*—and in a solemn tone, so very different from that of his handwritten letters—that he was calling this journey his third, "because it was preceded by two other journeys to the west, which I undertook in the service of the illustrious King of Spain" (*"Vostra Magnificenza saprá come per commissione de questo Re d'Ispagna mi partí"*). For to whom does he disclose this surprising news that he had already taken two journeys? To none other than the principal of his firm, whose representative and correspondent he had been for ten years and who thus must have known to the day and hour when his factor had embarked on long voyages, and whose business it was to keep in his books an exact account of the cost of the equipment and the profits. This would be as absurd as for an author, while posting the manuscript of a new book to his publisher who for years has published his work and kept his accounts, to enclose the surprising information that this is not his first book, and that he has published other books before.

Similar contradictions and inaccuracies can be found on almost every page in the printed text—contradictions and inaccuracies which in no instance can be traced back to Vespucci himself. Thus all probabilities confirm Magnaghi's theory that Vespucci's three handwritten letters, which were found in the archives and which so far had been declared spurious by Vespucci's defenders, represent in reality the only reliable material we possess from Vespucci's pen; while the famous works, the *Mundus Novus* and the *Quatuor Navigationes,* must be considered questionable publications because of their additions, alterations, and distortions at the hands of other people.

To be sure, to call the *Quatuor Navigationes* a falsification simply for these reasons would again be a gross exaggeration, for obviously authentic material from Vespucci's pen has gone into their making. What the unnamed editor did is more or less what happens in the antique business when a genuine piece of Renaissance furniture is manipulated into two or three pieces or an entire set by cunning use of the material and with the addition of simulated parts—a process which makes it as incorrect to insist that the furniture is genuine as to dub it a fake. The printer in Florence who carefully avoids mentioning his name on the title-page had no doubt obtained Vespucci's letters to the Medici bank—the three we know, and very likely others we do not know. Now, this printer was aware of the surprising success won by Vespucci's letter concerning his third journey, the *Mundus Novus,* for it had been printed no less than twenty-three times in fewer years, in all known languages! Nothing seems more natural, therefore, than that he who knew all the other reports from the original and from copies as well should be tempted to publish the *Collected Journeys* of Vespucci in a new small volume. But since the existing material was not sufficient to balance the four journeys of Columbus with the four by Vespucci, this unknown publisher decided to "stretch" the material. First of all he split up the report of the 1499 voyage into two, making one take place in 1497 and the other in 1499, without the remotest idea that by this deception he was branding Vespucci a liar and swindler for three centuries. What is more, from

other letters and reports of other sailors he patched on
details until this *mixtum compositum* of truth and lies
was achieved, which then for hundreds of years proceeded
to provide scholars with headaches and America with the
name America.

A doubter of this theory could perhaps ask if such an
impertinent usurpation were at all thinkable, that an author's work could be expanded by wilful inventions without his permission. Now, chance has it that we can prove
the existence of such an unscrupulous procedure actually
in connexion with Vespucci, for only one year later, in
1508, a fifth journey is invented in Vespucci's name (and,
incidentally, in the crudest fashion) by a Dutch printer.
Just as the unknown issuer of the *Four Journeys* derived
the material for his book from manuscript letters, so the
Dutch printer finds the desired opportunity for his forgery in the travel description of the Tirolean Balthasar
Sprenger, which was circulating in manuscript. In place
of the "ego, Balthasar Sprenger," he simply substitutes
"ick, Alberigus"—I, Amerigo—to deceive the public into
believing that this book of travel is derived from Vespucci.
And even four hundred years later the impertinent falsification has actually made a fool of the director of the

Amerigo

Geographical Society in London, a man who announced with great gusto in 1892 that he had discovered a fifth voyage by Vespucci.

Thus there is little doubt—and this clarifies the so far confused situation—that this fictitious report of the first journey, and all other inaccuracies of which Vespucci had been accused for so long, should be laid not at Vespucci's door, but at that of the unscrupulous publisher and printer, the man who, without asking Vespucci's permission, garnished his private travel reports with all manner of faked trimmings, finally releasing them in this form to the press. But against this interpretation, which clearly explains the situation, his opponents raise one last objection. Why, they ask, has Vespucci, who before his death in 1512 must have heard of these books attributing to his name a voyage he had never made, why has he never publicly protested against this ascription? Should it not have been his first duty, they ask, to hurl at the world a resounding: "No. I am not the discoverer of America! It is only by mistake that this country bears my name!"? Is not someone who refuses to protest against a swindle, because silence is advantageous to him, also implicated in the swindle?

Who Was Vespucci?

At first sight this objection looks convincing; but where, one is compelled to ask, could Vespucci have protested? At what court could he have raised his objection? In his day there was no notion of literary property. Everything written, everything printed, belonged to all, and everyone could use another's name and work as he pleased. Where could Albrecht Dürer have made protest that dozens of engravers signed their works with his customary signature "A.D."? Where could the authors of the first *King Lear* or of the original *Hamlet* go to object that Shakespeare had stolen their plays and deliberately altered them? Where, on the other hand, was Shakespeare to cry his disapproval of other people's plays appearing under his name? Where was even Voltaire to lodge his protest against the use of his world-famous name for mediocre, atheistic, and philosophical pamphlets? How could it have been possible, then, for Vespucci to institute proceedings against the dozens and dozens of publications of the *Collected Works,* all of which dragged his unearned fame throughout the world in increasingly distorted versions? All that remained for Vespucci was to vindicate his innocence in his personal circle by word of mouth.

That he did this is beyond doubt; for in 1508 or 1509,

at least, isolated copies of his books must have reached Spain. Now, is it likely that the King would have chosen for the responsible task of instructing his pilots in the drawing up of accurate and reliable reports a man who published false accounts about discoveries, if this man had not been able, personally, to free himself of all suspicion? What is still more important is that one of the first owners of the *Cosmographiæ Introductio* in Spain was, as has been proved (the copy with his comments still exists), Fernando Colombo, son of the admiral. He had not only read the book in which it is asserted in the face of all truth that Vespucci had set foot on the mainland before his father, but he even made notations in precisely this volume in which it was proposed for the first time to call the new country America. But what is strange is that while Fernando Colombo, in his biography of his father, attacks all manner of men for their envy of him, he has not so much as a single unkind word for Vespucci. Even Las Casas evinces surprise over this omission. "I am amazed," he writes, "that Don Hernando Colón, son of the Admiral and a man of sound judgment, who I happen to know was in possession of Amerigo's *Navigationes* failed to take any notice of the injustice and usurpation committed by Amerigo Vespucci against his illustrious father." But nothing speaks more revealingly for Vespucci's innocence than the son's silence over that unfortunate attribution which prevents his father from seeing his name given to the world he discovered: he must have known that it occurred without the knowledge or the desire of Vespucci.

As objectively as possible, chronologically from its origin, and through all its vicissitudes, we have tried to present here the "Causa Vespucci." The main problem to be solved centred on the strange conflict between a man and his fame, between a person and his name, for Vespucci's actual achievement does not correspond, as we know, to his fame, nor the fame to his achievement. The contrast between the man as he was and the man as he appeared to the world was so sharp that the two portraits, the one from life and the literary picture, could not merge. Only when we take into account that his fame was a product of interference from other people and of peculiar coincidences is it possible to regard his life and his real achievement as one, and to see them in proper relation to one another.

Amerigo

And thus emerges the rather modest result that the life of a man whose fame excited the admiration and indignation of the world as have few others has in reality been neither a great nor a dramatic one. It is not the biography of a hero, nor that of an impostor, but simply a comedy of accidents in which he had become innocently involved. Amerigo Vespucci was born in Florence, the third son of the notary Cernastasio Vespucci, on May 9, 1451, thus a hundred and thirty years after Dante's death. He comes of a distinguished though impoverished family, enjoying what in these circles is the customary humanistic education of the early Renaissance. He learns Latin, though admittedly without ever mastering its literary forms; from his uncle Fra Giorgio Vespucci, a Dominican monk at Saint Marco's, he acquires a smattering of science, mathematics and astronomy. Nothing in the young man is suggestive of any special talent or ambition. While his brothers are at the university, he is content with a commercial position in the Medici bank, which at that time is under the direction of Lorenzo de' Medici (not to be confused with his father, Lorenzo il Magnifico). So in Florence Amerigo Vespucci has not been considered a great man, and still less a great scholar. Preserved letters of his to his friends reveal him as preoccupied with petty business and unimportant private affairs. Nor as a merchant in the house of the Medici does he seem to have advanced very far, and it is only chance that brings him to Spain. Like the Welsers, the Fuggers, and the other German and Flemish merchants, the Medicis have branches of their firm in Spain and Lisbon. They finance expeditions to new countries, try to obtain information, and above all to invest their money in those places where at the moment it is most urgently needed. Now it appears that in the Medici office in Seville an employee has committed certain irregularities with money, and as Vespucci is considered by them—as by all others during his life— a particularly honest and reliable man, they send him, this insignificant employee, on May 14, 1491, to Spain, where he enters the banking-firm of Juanoto Beraldi, branch office of the Medici house. Here again, at Beraldi's, which is occupied mainly with the equipping of ships, his position is a completely subordinate one. Though in his letters he calls himself *"merciante fiorentino,"* he is by no means an independent merchant with his own capital and sphere of action, but merely a "factor" of Beraldi, who himself is only an employee of the Medici firm. Still, if

Amerigo

not in an exalted position, nevertheless Vespucci does acquire in time the personal confidence, even the friendship, of his employer. And in 1495, as Beraldi is nearing his death, he appoints Amerigo Vespucci executor of his last will, and it falls to him to liquidate the firm after Beraldi has died.

And so it happens that Amerigo Vespucci, approaching his fiftieth year, is suddenly left without means. Evidently he lacks both the capital and the inclination to continue Beraldi's business on his own account. What he has been doing in Seville during the following years of 1497 and 1498 can no longer be ascertained today, because of the complete lack of documents. Whatever he did—which is proved by the later letter of Columbus—he has not fared very well, and it is probably this absence of success which goes to explain the sudden change in his life. Twenty, almost thirty, years the efficient and industrious Florentine had wasted as a petty employee in foreign firms. He has neither home, wife, nor child; he stands alone in the world; middle age is upon him, and still nowhere does he see any sign of security or stability. Now this era of discovery offers unusual opportunities to the daring man prepared to stake his life on grasping fame and wealth at a single bold deal; it is a time for adventure and risks such as the world has never known again. And like hundreds and thousands of other stranded existences, the insignificant and probably bankrupt ex-merchant, Amerigo Vespucci, decides to try his luck on a voyage to the "New India." So in May 1499, when Alonso de Hojeda equips a fleet in the service of the Cardinal Fonseca, Amerigo Vespucci embarks with him.

In what capacity Alonso de Hojeda took him along is not quite clear. The factor of Beraldi's outfitting-firm has no doubt acquired a certain expert knowledge in his daily intercourse with captains, shipbuilders, and contractors. Apart from knowing a ship from stem to stern, as an educated Florentine he is also a hundredfold superior in intellectual calibre to his travelling companions, and already seems to have used his time for acquiring nautical knowledge. He learns how to use the astrolabe, the new methods of measuring longitude; he busies himself with astronomy, and practises the drawing of maps. Thus we can assume that he accompanied the expedition in the capacity of pilot or astronomer, and not as a simple broker.

But even if Amerigo Vespucci should not have accompanied the expedition as a pilot at that time, he at all events returns as a seasoned expert from this voyage of many months. Intelligent, a good observer, a practised mathematician, an inquisitive mind, a clever cartographer, he must in all these months have acquired special knowledge which made him most outstanding in seafaring circles. For, now that the King of Portugal is preparing a new expedition to the Brazilian region just discovered by Cabral, to whose northern coast Vespucci also sailed with Hojeda, it is to Vespucci he turns with the proposal of accompanying him on the new expedition as pilot, astronomer, and cartographer. The fact that the King of the neighbouring country, who certainly does not suffer from any lack of good pilots and seamen, should summon Vespucci to his assistance is proof conclusive of a special estimation of the so far unknown man.

Vespucci does not hesitate long. The voyage with Hojeda has not brought him any profit. After many months of hardship and danger, he has returned to Seville just as poor as when he started. He has no rank, no position, no fortune. Thus it is no disloyalty toward Spain when he answers this honourable call.

But neither does this new journey bring him profit, or even honour. For his name is mentioned as little in connexion with this expedition as is that of the commander of the fleet. The appointed task of this voyage of reconnaissance was exclusively to sail along the immense coast as far as possible in an attempt to find the longed-for strait leading to the Spice Islands. For the world is still steeped in the illusion that the Terra de Santa Cruz found by Cabral is nothing but an island of medium size, and that by circumnavigating it one would reach the Moluccas, the source of all wealth, El Dorado of the spices. It now becomes the historical merit of this expedition, which Vespucci accompanies, to have been the first one to correct this error. The Portuguese steer up the coast as far as the thirtieth, fortieth, and fiftieth degree of latitude, and still the country fails to come to an end. The torrid zones are far behind; it begins to grow colder, and colder, till finally they are compelled to abandon all hope of circumnavigating this vast new country, which bars their way to India like some gigantic cross-beam. But from this voyage, representing one of the most daring and imposing feats of its time, and during which Vespucci could proudly claim to have traversed a fourth part of the world, this one unknown man brings infinite gain to the science of geography: Vespucci conveys to Europe the knowledge that this newly discovered land is not India, not an island, but a *mundus novus*—a new continent, a new world.

Nor does the next journey—which Vespucci undertakes once more in the service of the King of Portugal and for the same purpose, that of finding the eastern route to India and thus trying to accomplish the feat destined for another, Magellan—achieve its aim. Though this time the fleet steers south and seems to have sailed far beyond the River La Plata, they are forced finally to return, driven back by storms. So once again Vespucci, now in his fifty-fourth year, lands in Lisbon, a poor, disappointed, and—as he thinks—completely unknown man, one of the countless ones who departed in search of fortune in the New India but failed to find it.

In the meantime, however, something had happened which Vespucci—under those other stars and on the globe's other hemisphere—could have neither guessed nor dreamed of. He, the poor little anonymous pilot, had created an uproar throughout the entire learned world. Each time he had returned from a voyage he had honestly and faithfully reported in letters to his former employer and personal friend, Lorenzo de' Medici, about what he had seen on his trip. He had, moreover, kept

Who Was Vespucci?

diaries which he handed over to the King of Portugal, and which, like his letters, being entirely private documents, were intended only for political and commercial information. Never had it crossed his mind to pose as a scholar or writer or to look upon these private letters as literary, much less learned, productions. He himself makes a point of stating that he finds all the things he has written *"di tanto mal sapore,"* and cannot bring himself to publish them as they stand. While mentioning the plan of a book, he adds that he would attempt it only "with the aid of learned men." Only with such help and on settling down and finding peace—*"quando saro de reposo"*—would he make an effort to write a book on his voyages, so as to win for himself a little fame—*"qualche fama"*—after his death. But without knowing, and certainly without meaning to, during these months on foreign seas he has acquired the reputation of being the most learned geographer of his time, and a great writer. Probably very freely edited, and composed in such a style as to suggest great learning, his letter to Lorenzo de' Medici had been translated into Latin; and hardly had it appeared in print under the title *Mundus Novus* before it created a tremendous sensation. Since these four printed pages have fallen on the world, it is known in all towns and ports that these newly discovered countries are not India, as Columbus believed, but a new world; and it is Alberigus Vespucius who is the first to announce this astounding fact. But the very man who throughout Europe is considered a scholar of great knowledge and the most daring of all navigators, is totally ignorant of his fame, and is trying very modestly to find at last a job which will enable him to lead a quiet and simple life. Having married beyond the prime of life, he is now definitely tired of business affairs, adventure, and travel. At last, in his fifty-seventh year, his desire is fulfilled, and he obtains what he has been looking for all his life: a modest, peaceful, frugal existence as chief pilot to the Casa de Contratación, with an income of at first fifty, and later seventy-five, thousand maravedis. From this moment on, the modern Ptolemy is but one among many other respected officials in Seville—nothing more, nothing less.

Did Vespucci ever know in these last years of his life how much fame had in the meantime been spun out of misunderstandings and errors round his name? Did he ever have any idea that the new land across the ocean had been called after his Christian name? Did he fight against this unjustified renown? Did he smile upon it, or merely, with discretion and modesty, let some of his most intimate friends know that nothing had happened precisely as it had been described in the books? Concerning all this we know only one thing, that this great hurricane roaring over mountains, oceans, countries, and languages, and already reaching the other, the New World, did not bring to his life the slightest profit of any tangible nature. Vespucci remains as poor as on the first day he set foot in Spain, so poor that after his death on February 22, 1512, his widow is compelled to petition supplicatingly for a pension of ten thousand maravedis a year, to provide for her barest needs. The only precious possessions left by him, the diaries of his travels, which alone could tell us the truth, fall to his nephew, who guards them so carelessly that they, like so many other priceless records of this age of discovery, are lost for ever. Nothing but a rather dubious fame, and that not altogether his due, remains of the toil of this modest and obscure existence.

One perceives, then, that this man who for four centuries offered for solution one of the most complicated problems led, at bottom, a quite uncomplicated and unproblematical life. For we may as well resign ourselves

to the fact that Vespucci was but a man of medium calibre, not the discoverer of America, not the "*amplificator
orbis terrarum.*" Nor was he, on the other hand, the liar
and swindler he has been called. Not a great writer, yet
not a man with any pretensions to be one. Not a scholar,
profound philosopher, or astronomer; not a Copernicus
or Tycho Brahe. It may be an exaggeration even to class
him in the first rank among great navigators and discoverers, for the unkindness of fate had denied him any
real initiative. Unlike Columbus and Magellan, he had
never been entrusted with a fleet. Always, in all profes-
sions, he was condemned to remain a subordinate, incapable of invention, command, or leadership. Always he
remained in the second rank, always in the shade of
others. If in spite of this the radiant light fell just on him,
it was not by reason of his special merit, or his particular
fault, but because of a combination of circumstances—
through error, accident, and misunderstanding. It could
just as well have struck another letter-writer on the same
voyage, or another pilot in a neighbouring ship. But history will not be reasoned with; it chose just him, and its
decisions, even those erroneous and unfair, are irrevocable.
With two words, *"Mundus Novus,"* with which he, or

Who Was Vespucci?

his unknown publisher, headed his letter, and by the *Four Journeys*—whether he undertook them all or not—he sailed into the haven of immortality. His name is not to be effaced from the glorious book of humanity, and his contribution to the history of mundane knowledge can perhaps be best described with the paradox that Columbus discovered America but failed to recognize it, while Vespucci did not discover it but was the first to recognize it as America, as a new continent. This one merit remains bound up with his life, his name. For it is never the deed alone that decides, but only its perception and effect. He who relates and explains it often becomes more important than the man who actually did it, and in the incalculable play of the forces in history often the slightest impetus is responsible for the most overwhelming results. Anyone expecting justice from history asks of it more than it is willing to give. Often it concedes achievement and immortality to the simple and mediocre man, casting the best, the most courageous, and the wisest, unmentioned into oblivion. Nevertheless, America has no cause to be ashamed of its name. It is the name of an honest and brave man, who in his fiftieth year ventured three times into the unknown on tiny boats across the

Amerigo

hitherto unexplored ocean, as one of those "unknown sailors" who risked their lives by the hundreds for danger and adventure. And perhaps the name of so undistinguished a person, of one of the anonymous crowd of the brave, is more fitting for a democratic country than that of a king or a conquistador, and certainly more just than if America had been called West India, New England, New Spain, or Holy Cross Land. It was not the will of a person that has carried this mortal name into immortality; rather it was the will of fate which remains always right, even when it seems to do wrong. Where this higher will commands, one can only acquiesce. And thus it is that today, as a matter of course, we use the word which in a capricious mood blind chance contrived as the only true and conceivable one: the echoing, resounding word America!

AMERIGO VESPUCCI

"From the celebrated Portrait of the Discoverer
painted from Life by Bronzino—always preserved
by the Vespucci family and by them committed to
C. Edwards Lester, Esq., U. S. Consul to Genoa."

[Portrait, copyright 1851, with description as above is in
the files of the New York Public Library]

Detail of Waldseemüller map (see endpaper) on which the newly discovered "Fourth Part" is first called "America."

Mundus Nouus

Albericus vespucius Laurentio
Petri de medicis salutem plurimam dicit.

Uperiozibus dieb⁹ satis ample tibi scripsi ꝺe reditu meo ab
nouis illis regionibus q̃s ꞇ classe ꞇ unpensis ꞇ mãdato isti⁹
serenissimi portugalie regis pᵭsiuimus ꞇ inuenim⁹: quasꝗ
nouũ mundũ appellare licet. Quando apud maiozes nᷓos
nulla ꝺe ipis fuerit habita cognitio ꞇ audientib⁹ oibus sit nouissima res.
Et eñ hec opinionẽ nostrox antiquo⅞ excedit: cũ illo⅞ maioz pars dicat
vltra lineã equinoctialẽ: ꞇ versus meridiem nõ esse ꝑtinentẽ: sed mare tan
tum qᴅ atlanticũ yocauere. ꞇ si qui coᴦ ꝑtinentẽ ibi eē affirmauerũt: eam
esse terrã habitabilẽ multis rõnibus negauerũt. Sed hanc eoᴦ opinionẽ
esse falsam ꞇ veritati omnino ꝑtrariã: hec mea vltima nauigatio ꝺeclara-
uit: cũ in ꝑtibus illis meridianis continentẽ inuenerim frequentiozibus
pplis ꞇ aialibus habitatã: q̃ nostrã europã seu asiam vel africã: ꞇ insuꝑ
aerẽ magis tempatũ ꞇ amenum q̃m in quauis alia regione a nobis cogni
ta pzout inferius intelliges: vbi succincte tantum re⅞ capita scribem⁹: ꞇ
res digniozes annotatione ꞇ memozia que a me vel vise vel audite in hoc
nouo mundo fuere⅟t infra patebit.

Rospero cursu quartadecima mensis maij millesimo q̃ngentesi
mo primo recessim⁹ ab olysippo mãdante prefato rege cũ tribus
nauibus ad inq̃rendas nouas regiones versus austrũ et viginti
mensibus ꝑtinẽter nauigauimus ad meridiẽ: cuius nauigationis
ozdo talis est. Nauigatio nᷓa fuit p̃ insulas fortunatas: sic olim ꝺictas
nunc aũt appellãtur insule magne canarie: que sunt in tertio climate ꞇ in
ꝑfinibus habitati occidentis. Inde p̃ oceanũ totum littus africum ꞇ par
tem ethiopici ꝑcurrimus vsꝗ ad ꝓmontoziũ ethiopum: sic a ptolomeo
ꝺictũ: qᴅ nunc a nᷓis appellaᵗ caput viride: ꞇ ab ethiopicis besegbice: ꞇ
regio illa mandinga gradib⁹, riiij. intra tozridã zonã a linea equinocti
ali versus septẽtrionẽ: que a nigris gẽtibus ꞇ pplis habitaᵗ. Ibi resump
tis viribus ꞇ necessarijs nostre nauigatõi: extulimus anchozas ꞇ exp̃an
dimus vel a ventis: ꞇ nostrũ iter p̃ uastissimũ oceanũ dirigentes versus
antarcticũ parũper p̃ occidentẽ infleximus p̃ ventũ qui vulturnus ꝺiciᵗ:
et a die qua recessimus a ꝺicto ꝓmontozio: duũ mensiũ ꞇ triũ die⅞ spatio
nauigauimus anteꝗ vlla terra nobis appareret. In ea aũt maris vastita
te qᴅ passi fuerimus: que naufragÿ picula ꞇ que cozpozis incõmoda susti
nuerimus: qᴃusꝗ anxietatibus animi laboᴦauerimus: existimationi coᴦ
relinquo: qui multaᴦ reᴦũ expientia optime norũt: qᴅ sit incerta querere
ꞇ que an si sint ignozãtes inuestigare: ꞇ vt vno verbo vniuersa pᵭstringaᵗ

scies quod ex diebus sexaginta septem quibus nauigauimus:continuos
quadraginta quatuor babuimus cū pluuia tonitruis z choruscatōibus
ita obscuros vt neqȝ solē in die:neqȝ serenū celū in nocte vnqȝ viderem⁹.
Quo factū est vt tātus in nobis incesserit timor:qȝ pene iam oēm vite spē
abieceram⁹:in his aūt tot tātisqȝ procellis maris z celi:placuit altissimo
nobis corā mōstrare ptinentē z nouas regiones ignotūqȝ mundū. Quibus visis tāto pfusi fuim⁹ gaudio:qȝtū quisqȝ cogitare pōt solere his accidere q ex varijs calamitatibus z aduersa fortuna salutem psecuti sunt
Die aūt septima augusti millesimo qngentesimo primo:in ipsaȝ regionū
littoribus submisim⁹ anchoras: grās agētes deo nfo solēi supplicatōe
atqȝ vnius misse cantu cū celebritate. Jbi eam terrā cognouim⁹ nō insulā
sed cōtinentē esse:quia z longissimis pducit littoribus nō ambientibus
eam:z infinitis babitatoribus repleta est. Mā in ea innumeras gentes z
pplos z oim siluestriū aialium genera:que in nostris regionibus reperi-
untur inuenim⁹: z multa alia a nobis nūqȝ visa:de qbus singulis longū
esset referre. Multa nobis dei clemētia circūfullit quādo illis regionib⁹
applicuimus:nam ligna defecerant z aqua:paucisqȝ diebus in mari vitā
pferre poteramus. Jpsi honor et gloria z gratiarūactio.

Ōnsilium cepimus nauigandi secundū hui⁹ ptinentis littus versus orientem:nūqȝ illius aspectū relicturi. Morqȝ illud tōdiu p-
currimus:qȝ puenim⁹ ad vnū angulū vbi litus versurā faciebat
ad meridiē: z ab eo loco vbi primū terrā attigimus vsqȝ ad būc angulū:
fuerūt circa trecente leuce:in buius nauigatōis spatio:pluries descendi-
mus in terrā:z amicabilr cū ea gente puersati fuim⁹:vt infra audies. Ob-
litus fuerā tibi scribere qȝ a pmōtorio capitis viridis vsqȝ ad pncipium
illi⁹ ptinentis: sunt circa septingente leuce: qȝuis existimē nos nauigasse
plusqȝ mille octingentas partim ignorāti a locor z naucleri:partim tēpe
statibus z ventis ipedientibus nostrȝ rectū iter:z ipellentibus ad freqn-
tes versuras.Quod si ad me socij animū nō adiecissent cui nota erat cosmographia: nullus erat nauclerus seu dux nauigatiōis:q ad qngentas
leucas nosceret vbi eēmus.Eramus em vagi z errātes:z instrumēta tan-
tūmodo altitudinū corporȝ celestiū:nobis ad amussim veritatē ostenderūt:
z hi fuere qdrans z astrolabiū:vti oēs cognouere. Hinc deiceps me oēs
mlto sunt bonore psecuti.Ostendi em eis qȝ sine cognitōe marine charte
nauigandi disciplinā magis callebā: qȝm oēs naucleri tocius orbis . Mā
hi nullā hūt noticiā:nisi eor locor que sepe nauigauerūt. Vbi aūt dictus
angul⁹ terre mōstrauit nobis versurā litoris ad meridiē: puenimus illud
pter nauigare:z inqrere qd in eis regionibus eēt. Nauigauim⁹ aūt secū-
dū littus circa sexcentas leucas z sepe descendim⁹ in terrā z colloqueba-
m ur z puersabamur cū eaȝ regionū colonis ab eisqȝ fraterne recipieba-

mur: ꝛ fecū qñꝗ moꝛabamur qndecim vel viginti dies cõtinuos amica-
biliter ꝛ hoſpitabilꝛ vt inferius intelliges. Moue iſtius cõtinentis pars
eſt in toꝛꝛida ʒona vltra lineã equinoctialē verſus polū antarcticū nã ei⁹
pncipiū incipit in. viij. ꝗ. vltra ipam eqnoctialē. Scōm huius litus tãdiu
nauigauim⁹ q̄ pꝛetergreſſo capꝛicoꝛni tropico inuenimus polū antarcticū illo coꝛ oꝛiʒont: altioꝛē. l. ꝗ. fuimuſꝗ ꝓpe ipſius antarctici circulū ad
ꝗ. xvij. ſemis ꝛ qd ibi viderim ꝛ cognouerim de natura illaꝛ gentiū deꝗ
eaꝛ moꝛib⁹ ꝛ tractabilitate de fertilitate terꝛe de ſalubꝛitate aeris de diſpo
ſitione celi coꝛpoꝛibuſꝗ celeſtibus et maxime de ſtellis fixis. viij. ſphere
nunꝗ a maioꝛibus noſtris viſis aut pꝛtractatis deinceps narabo.

Ⴖ Rimū igitur quo ad gentes tantã in illis regioibus gentis mul-
titudinē inuenim⁹ qntã nemo dinūerare poterat (vt legit in apo-
calipſi) gentē dico mitē atꝗ tractabilē oēs vtriuſꝗ ſexus incedūt
nudi: nullã coꝛpoꝛis parte opientes ꝛ vti ex ventre matris ꝓdcūt
ſic vſꝗ ad moꝛtē vadūt. Coꝛpoꝛa ēm habent magna qdrata bene diſpo
ſita ac ꝓpoꝛtionata ꝛ coloꝛe declinantia ad rubedinē qd eis accidere puto
quia nudi incedētes tingant a ſole. Habent ꝛ comã amplã ꝛ nigꝛa ſunt
in inceſſu ꝛ ludis agiles ꝛ liberali atꝗ venuſta facie quã tamen ipſimet
ſibi deſtruūt. Perfoꝛat ēm ſibi genas ꝛ labꝛa ꝛ nares ꝛ aures neꝗ credas
foꝛamia illa ēe pua aut q̄ vnū tantū habeãt. Vidi ēm nõnullos habētes
in ſola facie ſeptem foꝛamina quoꝛum quodlibet capax erat vnius pꝛuni
obturãt ſibi hec foꝛamina cum petris ceruleis marmoꝛeis criſtallinis et
ex alabaſtro pulcherrimis ꝛ cū oſſibus candidiſſimis ꝛ alijs rebus arti
ficioſe elaboꝛatis ſecūdum coꝛ vſum. Quod ſi videres rem tam inſolitã
ꝛ mōſtro ſimilem hoiem ſcz habentem in genis ſolum ꝛ in labꝛis ſeptem
petras quaꝛ nõnulle ſunt longitudinis palmi ſemis nõ ſine admiratiõe
eſſes. Sepe etēm pſideraui ꝛ iudicaui ſeptem tales petras eſſe ponderis
vnciaꝛ ſexdecim pter qd in ſingulis auribus trino foꝛamine perfoꝛatis
tenent alias petras pendentes in ãnulis ꝛ hic mos ſol⁹ eſt viroꝛ. Nam
mulieres nõ pfoꝛãt ſibi faciem ſed aures tantū. Alius mos eſt apud eos
ſatis enoꝛmis ꝛ pter oēm humanã credulitatē. Nã mulieres eoꝛ cū ſunt
libidinoſe faciūt intumeſcere maritoꝛ inguina in tantã craſſitudinem vt
defoꝛmia videant ꝛ turpia ꝛ ħ quodã eaꝛ artificio ꝛ moꝛdicatõe quoꝛū
dam aialium venenoſoꝛ ꝛ hui⁹ rei cauſa multi coꝛ amittūt inguina que
illis ob defectū cure fraceſcūt ꝛ reſtant cunuchi Nõ habent pannos neꝗ
lanceos neꝗ lineos neꝗ bombicinos quia nec eis indigent nec habent
bona ꝓpꝛia ſed oia cõmunia ſunt viuunt ſimul ſine rege ſine imperio et
vnuſquiſꝗ ſibi ipſi dñs eſt. Tot vxoꝛes ducūt q̄t volūt: ꝛ filius coit cum
matre ꝛ frater cū ſoꝛoꝛe ꝛ pmus cū pma ꝛ obuius cū ſibi obuia. Quoti-
ens volūt matrimonia dirimūt ꝛ in his nullū ſeruãt oꝛdinem. Pretereal

nullū hūt teplū z nullā tenēt legē neq̄ sunt idolatre: q̄d vltra dicā viuūt
scōm naturā z epicurei potius dici p̄nt q̄ stoici. Mō sunt inter eos mer=
catozes neq̄ cōmercia rex . Ppl'i inter se bella gerūt sine arte sine ozdine.
Sentozes suis q̄busdā cōtionibus iuuenes flectūt ad id q̄ volunt: z ad
bella incendūt in q̄bus crudeliter se mutuo interficiunt et quos ex bello
captiuos ducūt nō eox vite sed sui vict⁹ causa occidendos seruāt nā alij
alios et victozes victos comedunt z inter carnes humana est eis cōis in
cibis. Huius aūt rei certioz sis qz iam visum est patrē comedisse filios z
vxorē: z ego boiem noui quē z allocutus sum q̄ plusq̄x trecentis huma
nis cozpibus edisse vulgabat z itē steti dieb⁹ viginti septē in vrbe q̄dam
vbi vidi p domos humanā carnē salsam z cōtignatōibus suspensam vti
apud nos mozis est lardū suspendere z carnē suillam. Plus dico:ipsi ad
mirātur cur nos nō comedim⁹ inimicos nostros z eox carne nō vtimur
in cibis quā dicunt esse saporosissimā . Eox arma sunt arcus z sagitte : et
qn xperant ad bella nullā(sui tutandi gra) cozpis partem operiūt:adeo
sunt et in hoc bestijs similes . Mos q̄tum potuimus conati sumus eos
dissuadere z ab his prauis mozibus dimouere:q̄ z se eos dimissuros no
bis pmiserūt.Mulieres (vt dixi) z si nude icedāt z libidinosissime sint:
eax til cozpa satis formosa z munda:neq̄ tam turpes sunt q̄tum q̄s for=
san existimare posset:qz(qn carnose sunt) minus apparet eax turpitudo
que.s.pro maioziparte a bona cozpature qual.tate opta est.Mirū nobis
visum est q̄ inter eas nulla videbat que haberet vbera caduca:z que par
turierāt vteri forma z ptractura nihil distinguebant a v̄ginibus:z in reli
q̄s cozpor ptibus similia videbāt:que ppter honestatem cōsulto pterco.
Qñ se chzistianis iungere poterāt nimia libidine pulse:oēm pudicitiā cō
taminabāt atq̄ psituebant.Viuunt annis cētumqnquaginta:raro egro
tant:z siq̄ aduersam valitudinē incurrūt:seipsos cū quibusdā herbarū
radicib⁹ sanant . Hec sunt q̄ notabiliora apud illos cognoui.   Aer ibi
valde tempatus z bonus:z vt ex relatōe illox cognoscere potui:nunq̄ .ibi
pestis aut egrotatio aliqua que a corrupto pdeat aere z nisi morte violēta
moriant:longa vita viuunt credo qz ibi semp perflant venti australes et
maxime quē nos eurum vocam⁹:qui talis est illis qualis nobis est aqlo:
sunt studiosi piscature:z illud mare piscosum est et omn⁹ genere piscium
copiosum.Mō sunt venatozes:puto qz cū ibi sint multa aialium siluestri
um genera z maxime leonū z vrsox et inumerabilium serpentū aliarūq̄
hozriday atq̄ deformiū bestiay:z etiā cū ibi longe lateq̄ pateāt silue z im
mense magnitudinis arbozes nō audent nudi atq̄ sine tegminibus z ar
mis tant⁹ se discrimibus exponere.

Regionū illax terza valde fertilis est z amena:mltisq̄ collib⁹z mōtib⁹
z infinitis vallib⁹ atq̄ maximis fluminib⁹ abundās z salubzis fou

tibus irrigua:τ latissimis siluis τ densis vixᵹᶻ penetrabilibus:oĩ ᵹᶻ feraᵹ
genere plenis copiosa. Arbores maxime ibi sine cultore ꝓueniũt. Quaᵹ
multe fruct⁹ faciũt gustui delectabiles:τ bũanis corpibus vtiles:nõnu lle
vero ꝑtra:τ nulli fruct⁹ ibi bis nostris sunt similes. Gignũt etiã ibi in-
numerabilia genera herbaᵹ τ radicũ:ex ᵹbus pane conficiunt τ optima
pulmẽtaria: habẽt τ multa semina bis nostris oĩno dissimilia. Nulla ibi
metalloᵹ genera habent ꝑter auri: cui⁹ regiones ille exuberãt:licet nihil
ex eo nobiscũ attulerimus in hac ꝓima nostra nauigatiõe. Id nobis notũ
fecere incole:ᵹ affirmabãt in mediterraneis magnã esse auri copiã τ nihil
ab eis estimari vel in ꝓcio haberi. Abundãt margaritᵹ:vti alias tibi scripsi Si singula que ibi sunt cõmemorare:τ de numerosis aialium generib⁹
coᵹᵹᶻ multitudine scribere vellem : res esset oĩno ꝓlixa et imensa:τ certe
credo ᵹᶻ Plinius noster millesimã partem nõ attigerit generis psittacoᵹ:
reliquaᵹ auiũ nec nõ τ aialium que in ijsdem regionibus sunt cũ tanta
facieᵹ atᵹᶻ coloᵹ diuersitate : ᵹᶻ ꝓsũmate picture artifex policletus in pin
gendis illis deficeret. Dẽs arbores ibi sunt odorate:et singule ex se gumi
vel oleũ vel liᵹrem aliquem emittũt. Quoᵹ ꝓꝑrietates si nobis note essẽt:
nõ dubito quin humanis corpibus saluti foᵹrent:τ certe si padisus terre-
stris in aliᵹ sit terre pte:nõ longe ab illis regionib⁹ distare existimo. Quaᵹ
situs : vt dixi: est ad meridiem in tanta aeris temperie:ᵹᶻ ibi neᵹᶻ biemes
gelide:neᵹᶻ estates feruide vnᵹᶻ habentur.

Celũ τ aer a maxima pte anni serena sunt:τ crassis τ vaporibus inania.
Pluuie ibi minutim decidũt:τ trib⁹ vel ᵹtuor horis durãt:atᵹᶻ ad
instar nimbi euanescũt. Celũ spectosissimis signis τ figuris ornatũ est:in
quo annotaui stellas circiter viginti tante claritatis ᵹ̃te aliᵹ vidimus
Venerẽ τ Iouem. Maᵹ τ motus τ circuitões ꝓsideraui:earũᵹᶻ periꝑhe-
rias et diametros geometricis methodis dimensus sũ: easᵹᶻ maioris
magnitudinis eẽ deprehendi. Vidi in eo celo tres canopos:duos ᵹdem
claros:tertiũ obscuᵹ. Polus antarcticus nõ est figuratus tũ vrsa maiore
τ miõre:vt hic noster videt arcticus:nec iuxta eũ ꝓspicit aliᵹ clara stella:
ex his ᵹ circũ eũ breuiore circuitu feruntur tres sunt habetes trigoni ortho
goni schema:Quaᵹ dimidia piꝑherie diametrus: gradus habet nouem
semis. Cũ bis orientib⁹ a leua ꝓspicit vnus canop⁹ albus eximie magni
tudinis:que cũ ad mediũ celũ ꝓueniũt:banc habent figuram.

Post has veniūt alie due q̄rū dimidia pipherie diametr̄ gradus ha=
bet duodecim semis: z cum eis p̄spiciū alius canopus albus. His
succedūt alie sex stelle formosissime z clarissime inter ōes alias octaue sphe
re: q̄ in firmamētu supficie dimidia habent pipherie diametrū graduū tri
ginta duoq̄: cū his puolat ynus canopus niger imense magnitudinis:
p̄spiciunt in via lactea z bimōt figurā habēt qr̄ sunt i meridionali linea.

```
                       *                        Canopus
    *       *        *        ss
                            ssss            *
                          ssssss
                           ssss
                                    *
```

Multas alias stellas pulcerrimas cognoui: quar motus diligent
annotaui: z pulcerrime in quodā meo libello graphice descripsi
in hac mea nauigatōe. Nunc aūt impsentiar̄ tenet hic serenissim9
rex quē mihi restituturꝝ spero. In illo hemisperio vidi res philosophoꝛū
rōnibus nō p̄sentiētes. Iris alba circa mediā noctem bis visa est: nō solū
a me: sed etiā ab oibus nautis. Similiter planres nouā lunā vidimus eo
die quo soli piungebat: singulis noctibus in illa celi parte discurrūt in=
nueri vapores z ardentes faces. Dixi paulo ante: in illo hemisperio: q̄d
tamen ꝓprie loquēdo nō est ad plenū hemisperiū respectu nostru: quia ta=
men accedit ad huiusmodi formā: sic illud appellari licuit.
Igitur (vt dixi) ab olysippo vn digressi sumus: q̄d ab linea equi=
noctiali distat gradibus triginta noue semis: nauigauimus vltra
linea equinoctiale per q̄nquaginta gradus: q̄ simul iuncti efficiūt
gradus circiter nonaginta: que summa cū quartā parte obtineat summi
circuli secundū verā mensure rationē ab antiq̄s nobis tradita: manifestū
est nos nauigasse q̄rtā mundi parte. Et hac rōne nos olysippū habitan=
tes citra linea equinoctiale gradu trigesimo nono semis in latitudine se=
ptentrionali: sumus ad illos qui gradu quinq̄gesimo habitāt vltra eaū=
dem lineā in meridionali latitudine angulariter gradus quinq̄ in linea
transuersali: z vt clarius intelligas. Perpēdicularis linea que dum recti
stamus a puncto celi iminente vertici nostro depen det in caput nostrum:
illis depēdet in latus: z in costas. Quo fit vt nos simus in linea rectā: ip̄
vero in linea transuersa: z species fiat trianguli orthogonii: cui9 vicem li=
nee tenemus cathete: ip̄si aūt basis: z hypotenusa a nostro ad illoꝝ ꝑten=
ditur verticem vt in figura patet: z hec de cosmographia dicta sufficiāt.

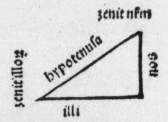

Hec fuerunt notabiliora que viderim in hac mea vltima nauigatõe quam appello diem tertiu. Mã alij duo dies fuerũt due alie nauigationes quas ex mandato sereniſſimi hiſpaniarum regis feci verſus occidentẽ in qbus annotaui mirãda ab illo ſublimi oim creatore deo noſtro pfecta: rex notabiliũ diar iũ feci: vt ſi qñ mihi ociũ dat ik: poſſim oia hec ſingularia atq mirabilia colligere: z vel geographie vel coſmographie hbꝝ pſcribere: vt mei reccordatio apud poſteros viuat: z oipotentis dei cognoſcat tam imenſum artificium in parte priſcis ignotũ nobis aũt cognitũ. Oro itaq clementiſſimũ deũ q mihi dies vite proget vt cũ ſua bona grã atq aie ſalute huius mee volũtatis optimã diſpoſitõem pficere poſſim. Alios duos dies in ſanctuarijs meis ſeruo: z reſtituẽte mihi hoc ſereniſſimo rege diem tertiũ patriã z quietẽ repetere conabor: vbi z cũ peritis cõferre z ab amicis ad id opus pficiendũ conſortari z adiuuari valeã.

A Te veniã poſco ſi nunc vltimã hanc meã nauigatiõem: ſeu poti? vltimũ diem tibi non tranſmiſi vti poſtremis meis litteris tibi pollicitus fuerã. Cauſam noſti qñ necdũ ab hoc ſereniſſimo rege archetypum habere potui. Mecum cogito adhuc efficere quartũ diem z hoc ptracto z iam mihi duarũ nauium cũ ſuis armamẽtis piniſſio facta eſt vt ad pquirendas nouas regiones verſus meridiẽ a latere oriẽtis me accingã per ventũ qui africus dr. In quo die multa cogito efficere in dei laude z huius regni vtilitatẽ: z ſenectutis mee honorem: z nihil aliud expecto niſi huius ſereniſſimi regis conſenſum. Deus id permittat quod melius eſt: quid fiet intelliges.

Ex italica in latinam linguam iocũdus interpres hãc epiſtolam vertit vt latini oẽs intelligant qz multa mirãda in dies reperiant z eoꝝ compꝛima tur audacia qui celũ et maieſtatem ſcrutari: et plus ſapere qz liceat ſapere volunt: quando a tanto tempore quo mundus cepit ignota ſit vaſtitas teꝛre z quecontineãtur in ea.

Laus Deo.

Lettera di Amerigo vespucci delle isole nuouamente trouate in quattro suoi viaggi.

THE SODERINI LETTER, 1504

Facsimile of the

Hoe-McCormick copy in Princeton University Library

ᗰAGNIFICe do
mine.Dipoi del
la humile reue
rentia & debite recõmenda
tioni &c̃ . Potra essere che
uostra Magnificentia simara
uigliera della mia temerita/
et usada uostra sauidoria/cõ
tãto absurdamẽte io mimuo
ua a scriuere a uostra Mag.
la psente lettera tãto plissa:
sappiendo che di cõtinuo uo
stra Mag. sta occupata nelli
alti consigli & negotii sopra
elbuon reggimẽto di cotesta
excelsa Repub. Et mi terra nõ solo presumptuoso / sed etiam
perotioso / in pormi a scriuere cose nõ conuenienti a uostro
stato / ne dilect euoli / & cõ barbaro stilo scripte / & fuora do
gni ordine di humanita:ma la cõfidentia mia che tengho nel
le uostre uirtu & nella uerita del mio scriuere/che son cose nõ
sitruouano scripte ne p li antichi ne p moderni scriptori / co
me nel pcesso conoscera V.M.mifa essere usato.La causa prin
cipale cñ mosse a scriuerui / fu p ruogho del psente aportato
re / che sidice Benuenuto Benuenuti nostro fiorẽtino / molto
seruitore secõdo che sidimostra / di uostra Mag. & molto ami
co mio:elquale trouandosi qui in questa citta di Lisbona / mi
prego che io facessi parte a uostra Mag.delle cose per me uiste
in diuerse plaghe del mondo / per uirtu di quattro uiaggi che
ho facti in discoprire nuoue terre:edua per mando del Re di
Castiglia don Ferrãdo Re.vi.per el gran golfo del mare ocea
no uerso loccidente:et laltre due p mandato del poderoso Re
don Manouello Re di Portogallo / uerso laustro:Dicendomi
che uostra Mag.nepiglierebbe piacere / & che in q̃sto speraua
seruirui:ilperche midisposi a farlo:pche mirendo certo cñ uo
stra Mag.mitiene nel numero de suoi seruidori / ricordãdomi
come nel tempo della nostra giouentu ui ero amico / & hora
seruidore:& andando a udire eprincipii di grãmatica sotto
la buona uita & doctrina del uenerabile religioso frate di. S.
Marco fra Giorgio Antonio Vespucci:econsigli & doctrina
delquale piacesse a Dio che io hauessi seguitato:che come dice